JUTLAND

Jutland

AN EYE-WITNESS ACCOUNT
OF A GREAT BATTLE

assembled and edited by
STUART LEGG

THE JOHN DAY COMPANY

New York

Contents

Foreword

LIKE its predecessor *Trafalgar*, this book makes no claim to scholarship. It is intended only as a story of action.

It is a book of quotations. In its making, written records of Jutland have been treated as raw material for marshalling and editing into a dramatic presentation of the battle—as a film is shaped by the ordering and cutting of the shots taken by the cameras.

To assist the flow of the action explanatory sub-headings have been kept to a minimum, and certain quotations have been shortened within the excerpts chosen, though without distortion of their sense. The numbers at the ends of quotations refer to sources correspondingly numbered at the end of the book.

No less than 250 warships were engaged at Jutland; and during the battle ships or groups of ships were frequently involved in episodes subsidiary to the main action. Moreover, the tactics of the battle, complex in themselves, afterwards became the subject of lasting controversy in which specific events, and the times of their occurrence, came to be regarded as essential evidence for particular schools of thought. To attempt to include all such episodes and events in a book of this kind would be to lose narrative thread and a sense of proportion. Thus, for example, the valiant exploits of the British destroyer *Onslow* under Commander Tovey, the torpedoing of the battleship *Marlborough*, Beatty's much-debated signal 'Submit van of battleships follow battle-cruisers,' made just before dusk on 31 May, and the mining of the German *Ostfriesland*, have been omitted as not affecting the central issue.

For such omissions the indulgence of experts is sought. They have been made solely in the interests of perspective on those crowded, crucial hours when the greatest fleets in naval history met in combat for the only time during their existence.

THE BRITISH GRAND FLEET

THE BATTLE-CRUISER FLEET

6 Battle-Cruisers   *Flagship:* Lion
(Vice-Admiral Sir David Beatty)

4 Fast Battleships

14 Light Cruisers

27 Destroyers

1 Seaplane Carrier

THE BATTLE FLEET

24 Battleships   *Flagship:* Iron Duke
(Admiral Sir John Jellicoe, Commander-in-Chief)

3 Battle-Cruisers

8 Cruisers

12 Light Cruisers

50 Destroyers

1 Minelayer

1 Auxiliary

151 ships

THE GERMAN HIGH SEAS FLEET

THE BATTLE-CRUISER FORCE

5 Battle-Cruisers   *Flagship:* Lützow
(Vice-Admiral Franz von Hipper)

5 Light Cruisers

30 Destroyers

THE BATTLE FLEET

22 Battleships   *Flagship:* Friedrich der Grosse
(Vice-Admiral Reinhard Scheer, Commander-in-Chief)

6 Light Cruisers

31 Destroyers

99 ships

Details of ships, squadrons and flotillas will be found at the end of the book.

Background to the Battle

In October 1805 Nelson and Collingwood had smashed the combined sea-power of France and Spain at Trafalgar. Thereafter, the oceans were empty of serious challenge to the strength of the Royal Navy. With her new industrial energy added to her mastery of the seas, Britain could impose upon the nineteenth century her pattern of colonially-based world trade.

But if Trafalgar was a triumph for Britain, it was little short of a disaster for the Navy which won it. Total victory led to complacency; and complacency to forgetfulness of ultimate purpose. As decade succeeded decade of peace, the outlook of the Victorian Navy changed from that of a tough, warlike service to the burnished smoothness of an ample police force in a law-abiding world.

Its seamanship was superb; its standards of smartness incomparable. But these concealed beneath the surface a moribund institution in which procedure and punctilio had replaced hard thinking and effective action. Spit and polish became a substitute for battle-readiness; fleet drills of ballet-like intricacy for tactical training; athletic fanaticism for the gunnery practice which dirtied brass and paint. To a dangerous extent ward-rooms became the hidebound preserve of county families, where instant obedience was the ladder to promotion and unsought initiative tantamount to insubordination. Responsibility towards the lower deck became an arrogant paternalism, enforced by discipline as pointless and living conditions as poor as the times allowed. To officers bred to the white beauty of sail, the advent of steam was first the Deluge, then a continuing squalor. Engineers were "greasers"; and "Coaling, Coaling, Coaling," sung to the dirge-tune of "Holy, Holy, Holy," sometimes marked the grimy process of bunkering. In the early twentieth century the order book of the Channel Fleet comprised 600 pages of minutely detailed dogma, drawn up to cover every contingency—except a war launched by an enemy whose mind worked in new terms.

Such, beneath the reassuring splendour of sparkling varnish, sounding bugles, bunting-laden halliards, was the British fleet when Wilhelm II dropped the Pilot and the German Navy Laws of 1898 and 1900 were promulgated. The aim of the Navy Laws was explicit in their preamble: to create a fleet so powerful that "if the strongest naval power engaged it, it would endanger its own supremacy." The political reasons for its building became clear in incidents like the Kruger Telegram and the successive crises of Morocco, Casablanca and Agadir. Germany was entering the competition for empire, and her fleet would be a means to secure her place in the colonial sun. Though the implications were disturbing, it was difficult at first for Britain to assess her new maritime rival objectively. The British fleet was by far the largest afloat. More important, it had behind it a formidable tradition of sea supremacy stretching back to the Tudors, and crowned by the century of the Pax Britannica that had followed Trafalgar. It seemed that the problems which would confront a continental landpower in building, from the keel up and in a few years, a navy capable of confronting such strength might prove insuperable.

Only by a relatively small circle in the Admiralty was the true calibre of the German naval effort discerned at the outset. This group of younger British officers had begun to emerge at the turn of the century around the person of Admiral Fisher, who was in command of the Mediterranean Fleet when the German Navy Laws were passed. Acutely aware of the hidden decay within the Royal Navy, they formed themselves, as they achieved senior rank, into what was virtually a school to carry through a crash programme of reform. Their chance came when Fisher was appointed First Sea Lord on 21 October 1904—the day of the 99th anniversary of Trafalgar.

Fisher was one of the most fascinating and controversial figures in naval history. During his five years as professional head of the Navy he was variously described as "a mixture of Machiavelli and a child," "unscrupulous, half-Asiatic," and "ruthless, remorseless, relentless." He would sign letters "Yours till hell freezes." He would enter the parties of society ladies dancing a hornpipe. He would sit for hours alone in Westminster Abbey, hunched in meditation. He said of himself: "I entered the Navy penniless, friendless and forlorn. I have had to fight like hell, and fighting like hell has made me what I am." His fight was to bring the British Navy forward a century in the few years it would take Germany to launch and perfect her High Seas Fleet. "The only thing in the world that England has to fear is Germany."

He evolved a scheme for selecting officer cadets at the age of 12 and training them within the Navy. One of its aims was to raise the status of engineers;

and a bitter opposition described it as a means of "making greasers of us all." He examined the huge, obsolescent collection of ships and weapons which formed the Navy's equipment, and embarked on a wholesale programme of scrapping. He redistributed the fleet on a basis of strategic "not sentimental" needs, and concentrated three-quarters of its battleship strength in the home waters directly threatened by Germany. He established a Reserve Fleet with permanent nucleus crews which included all the specialists. In 1902 a British admiral had dismissed submarines as "underhand, unfair, and damned unEnglish." Fisher was certain that underwater craft and weapons would revolutionise sea warfare, and supported their development to the utmost.

His most fundamental reforms, however, revolved around the new types of capital ships that he and his associates introduced. Battleships had only one ultimate purpose: to destroy the enemy's battleships. Therefore, the ideal battleship would be capable of bringing the heaviest possible weight of broadside to bear at the longest possible range. All other considerations were secondary. Hitherto, no British battleship had carried more than four big guns, together with a large number of guns of smaller calibre. In the *Dreadnought*, launched by Edward VII at Portsmouth in 1906, Fisher pioneered the all-big-gun capital ship. *Dreadnought* was the first turbine-driven battleship, and had a speed of 21 knots—2 knots faster than any other battleship afloat. And she had a main armament of 10 12-inch guns. Horrified critics exclaimed that she was so revolutionary as to render all existing ships obsolete; she would be copied at once, and Britain's advantage in numbers and tonnage would evaporate. Fisher held that such ships were bound to come anyway, and that Britain should get in first. In subsequent classes of dreadnoughts the size and range of guns and the weight of the broadside they fired was steadily increased until Churchill, becoming First Lord in 1911, decided to cap them all with a division of fast super-dreadnoughts mounting eight guns of the unprecedented calibre of 15 inches. They were to be capable of 24 knots, and were to be the first oil-fired battleships in the British fleet. On completion these five ships formed the famous *Queen Elizabeth* class.

If the enemy's battle-fleet was to be destroyed, it must first be found. Reconnaissance was the task of cruisers: but owing to their relatively low speed and light armour, most cruisers were vulnerable and might be driven off. Fisher's group conceived of a ship which would be fast and powerful enough to keep observational contact in face of heavy hostile fire, and also to provide rapid reinforcement to any battleships requiring it during a general action. Her high speed and heavy armament would also enable her to hunt down commerce raiders. Because she would be something of a hybrid between a battleship and a cruiser, they called this new type of ship the battle-cruiser. *Invincible*, the first British battle-cruiser, was completed in 1908. She carried 8 12-inch guns, and 16 4-inch guns for defence against torpedo craft. Her top speed was 26·6 knots. Her design, and that of her successors, involved the deliberate sacrifice of protective armour, with its massive weight, in order to gain speed. Fisher believed that "speed is armour".

To give maximum effect to his big-gun fleet, Fisher fostered a new system of gunnery control known as Director Firing. This was the development of one of his group, Rear-Admiral Percy Scott. Till then, the fire of the guns was controlled by the gunlayers of individual guns or turrets, range and deflection being adjusted from their observation of the splashes caused by the shells striking the sea. Scott argued that with increased ranges, spotting from gun-housings at deck level would no longer be feasible; and even at closer ranges the larger number of guns firing would make it impossible for a gunlayer to identify his own splash. Greater speeds might result in more funnel smoke; and what with more cordite smoke from more guns and the chance of haze, gunlayers might be virtually blinded. Also, the new need was to concentrate salvo fire on selected targets. Scott's system transferred responsibility for shell-splash observation to a single spotting officer sitting in the "fore-top" or "fighting-top" high up in the foremast, as far above the waterline as possible and clear of obscuring smoke. He would report his observations by telephone to a transmitting station deep in the ship, where correcting calculations could be made behind thick armour and in relative quiet. These would be passed to all the guns, and the next salvo would be fired by a master-gunlayer or director, also located in the fore-top and equipped with telescopic sights. Director Firing was first installed in the battleship *Neptune* in 1911; but despite obviously improved results a long struggle was necessary before its opponents would accept it as standard equipment.

How would the reformed Navy fight, should the enemy accept a general engagement? Its core would be the battleships: the massive floating gun-platforms, moving ponderously through the sea, on whose capacity to destroy their opposite numbers while remaining intact themselves the fortunes of Britain and her world interests might depend. If time allowed before war came, upwards of 20 battleships might be available for a fleet action, probably divided into squadrons of eight each. While cruising at sea the battle-squadrons would normally steam in parallel columns, since this formation, screened all round by cruisers and destroyers, would give the best protection from torpedo-boats and submarines. But on warning of the enemy fleet's approach, it was expected that the battleships would form into a single line, one squadron being ordered to take the lead, and the others falling into place behind it until the long column, extending over several miles, was complete. This manœuvre was known as "deployment"; and it might be simple or complicated to execute according to the direction desired for the fighting column, the order of the squadrons, and the speed of the fleet. The aim of the Commander-in-Chief would be to deploy in such a way that his whole column of battleships would steam across the head of the enemy's column. This was called "Crossing the T". If achieved, it would ensure that all the big guns of the British battleships, moving round in their turrets, could be brought to bear on the leading ships of the enemy, wrecking them and throwing his line into confusion; while his ships could only open fire with their forward guns at a long, strung-out line. Clearly, if the enemy's T was to be crossed successfully, the manner and direction of deployment was vital, since the battle-line might take up to 20 minutes to form. The decision as to how, and in which direction, to deploy would therefore be the supreme test of the Commander-in-Chief's judgment; and much would depend, especially if visibility were poor, on his being kept fully informed by his scouting forces of the whereabouts and course of the enemy's fleet.

The principle of the single fighting line had first been applied during the wars with Holland in the seventeenth century, when it was necessary to impose order and cohesion on a number of heavy, cumbersome sailing-ships during the critical opening phases of a battle. Down to the Napoleonic Wars it was given doctrine; and it persisted into the twentieth century, despite the revolution of steam and science, largely because so long a period of peace had provided no opportunity for testing its continued validity. It had serious disadvantages: it limited the speed of all the battleships to that of the slowest; it was rigid to the point of removing all initiative from squadron commanders; and, once adopted, it offered little chance to change tactics quickly should the enemy's movements demand it. Indeed, some of the Navy's most cherished victories—Finisterre, Quiberon Bay, the Battle of the Saints, the Glorious First of June, and, not least, Trafalgar itself—had been won by deliberate departure from the line system in favour of manœuvre, divisional attack, and chase. All along, the line-versus-manœuvre debate had reflected a struggle in higher naval circles between orthodoxy and heresy. The line was the method of the conservative hierarchy: it was established; it obviated the need for original thought; it required only obedience from subordinates. And as soon as the radicals like Howe, Rodney and Nelson were off the stage, the conservatives closed their grip again. In the early twentieth century, Fisher—strangely, for a man who took so little for granted—accepted the line principle; and so did Admiral Jellicoe, one of his team and then Naval Controller in charge of ship design and ordnance. Younger rising officers like Beatty and Sturdee argued that it was out of date; that battles should now be approached in terms of the more fluid tactics which modern speed and manœuvrability made possible. But this junior school, who believed that rules are made to be broken by initiative and that victories may hang on the insight of the moment, had little say in the years of preparation against Germany. The emphasis was on *matériel*.

The new *matériel* was not without weaknesses, as Jellicoe, with his expert technical knowledge, was aware. Jellicoe doubted whether the quality of British protective armour was as good as the German; and he was particularly disturbed by the thin armour of the battle-cruisers. He was apprehensive of the new underwater menace: torpedoes launched against the fleet by fast torpedo-boats or invisible submarines; mines sown in permanent fields or strewn indiscriminately by a hostile fleet during a pursuit. He was conscious that the British fleet was neither equipped nor trained for fighting at night. Shortly before the outbreak of war he made a detailed comparative study of the British and German capital ships. One of his findings was that "the inferiority of the protection of the British ships of 1909–1911 classes against guns and torpedoes is very striking." And he concluded that "assuming equality in design it is highly dangerous to consider that our ships as a whole are superior or even equal fighting machines."

So the rival armadas grew. In the Spring of 1912 the Reichstag passed a Supplementary Navy Law to step up the German–British ratio of capital ships to 2 : 3. In the two subsequent years Britain enlarged her building programme to increase her lead. By July 1914 she possessed 29 dreadnoughts, the most up-to-date being armed with 13·5-inch guns. Eighteen more, including the 15-inch fast battleships, were on the stocks. Germany had 20 dreadnoughts in commission, with a maximum gun calibre of 12 inches, and seven more under construction. Nothing comparable with these two monstrous armaments, whose main purpose was to annihilate each other, had existed before. No one could accurately estimate what would happen if and when they met in battle. But it was generally believed that if the trial of power came, it would come in the North Sea.

Fisher had always seen Jellicoe as "Admiralissimo when Armageddon comes." Immediately on the outbreak of war he was appointed Commander-in-Chief of the Grand Fleet. His flagship *Iron Duke*, together with the majority of all British warships, was based at Scapa Flow, the bleak, lonely, natural harbour in the Orkneys guarding the northern exit from the North Sea, where the surrounding islands afforded protection against U-boats. Later, and largely to stiffen public morale against German hit-and-run raids on the East Coast towns of England, he moved a squadron of battleships south to Invergordon on Cromarty Firth, and the Battle-Cruiser Fleet under Vice-Admiral Sir David Beatty, flying his flag in *Lion*, to Rosyth on the Firth of Forth. Across the North Sea, the German High Seas Fleet was based on Wilhelmshaven, at the mouth of the Jade River. After various changes, Vice-Admiral Reinhard Scheer took over its command, with Vice-Admiral Franz von Hipper as leader of the German battle-cruiser force, known as the First Scouting Group.

Jellicoe's aim was to induce the High Seas Fleet to sea so that he could fall upon it with the full weight of his superior force; but only in circumstances where the risk to the Grand Fleet, and especially to its battleship squadrons, was minimal. A British victory, involving the destruction of the High Seas Fleet, would not crucially impair Germany's total power to wage war: a defeat, resulting in the loss of a significant number of her dreadnoughts, might bring Britain to her knees. Jellicoe felt, as Churchill afterwards wrote, that "he was the only man on either side who could lose the war in an afternoon"; and he believed it his first duty to conserve at all costs the fleet on which such enormous issues hung.

Scheer's problem was different. He knew that if he were to be confronted by Jellicoe's entire strength, the High Seas Fleet had little chance of survival; and he had carefully practised his battle squadrons in a number of evasive tactical movements specially designed to meet this perilous situation should it ever arise—movements which were unknown in the British fleet. If he took the offensive, it must be in such a way as to bring out against himself only a part of Jellicoe's strength at a time. With one or two successful actions of this kind, he could hope to wear down the British numbers to parity with his own—and then perhaps to fight it out later on equal terms.

In the first half of 1916 there were good reasons why the German fleet should play a more offensive role. The Kaiser's naval advisers had been demanding his permission to begin unrestricted submarine warfare against all merchant shipping heading for British ports. But the sinking of the *Lusitania* and the *Sussex*, both carrying American passengers, had aroused United States opinion; and he felt compelled to order its postponement. At the same time the terrible slaughter of the German armies at Verdun was bringing no visible reward. All over Germany morale was sagging. A naval victory could do much to restore it.

Scheer judged that another raid on the East Coast was the best way to lure the British into the North Sea at squadron rather than fleet strength. The springboard of his plan would therefore be a raid on Sunderland. Hipper and the German battle-cruisers would bombard the town; and meanwhile a force of U-boats would be stationed off the Grand Fleet's bases to attack the British ships as they came out to drive him off. Scheer himself, with the whole strength of the High Seas Fleet, would be in the North Sea, ready to meet any British squadrons which evaded the U-boats and were pursuing Hipper on his homeward journey.

It was possible, however, that the Grand Fleet might be out at the time; for Jellicoe made periodic sweeps southward from Scapa Flow to keep the North Sea clear for British merchant ships. An accidental meeting with the whole British fleet would be disastrous; and Scheer arranged to guard against it by zeppelin reconnaissance before the High Seas Fleet left Wilhelmshaven. But zeppelins could only leave their sheds in fine weather. So Scheer formed an alternative plan. If the weather was bad, Hipper, instead of bombarding Sunderland, would go northward from Wilhelmshaven as though to attack British shipping off the coasts of Denmark and Norway. His presence would be reported to Scapa Flow; British units would be sent to attack him; and

Scheer with the High Seas Fleet would come north in Hipper's wake to engage them.

On 15 May 1916 the U-boats left for their stations off Scapa Flow, Invergordon and Rosyth. Shortly afterwards, bad weather set in. Within two weeks Scheer would have to put one or other of his plans into operation, as by that time the U-boats would be running low on fuel and would have to return to port. The weather continued unfavourable, and the zeppelins could not leave their base. Scheer decided, therefore, to fall back on his second plan—that of going north towards the Skagerrack; and on 30 May he ordered Hipper to precede the High Seas Fleet out of Wilhelmshaven.

In the meantime it had become clear to the British Admiralty that German movements of an unusual kind were afoot. A number of U-boats had been sighted in the North Sea which did not appear to be molesting passing ships. On the morning of 30 May, intercepted wireless messages suggested abnormal activity in the Jade River. Then, about five o'clock in the afternoon, the British monitoring service picked up a German signal reading: "31 Gg 1490". This was undecipherable; but there was reason to believe that it was an operational order. The Admiralty waited no longer. At 5.40 p.m. a signal was sent to Jellicoe at Scapa Flow and to Beatty at Rosyth, ordering them to leave harbour with all their forces and concentrate to the eastward of the Long Forties, an area of the North Sea about 60 miles off the Scottish coast.

The Battle

"Fleet leaving 9.30 p.m. today."

Admiralty to:

Commander-in-Chief, Scapa Flow (Admiral Sir John Jellicoe)
Repeated to
Senior Officer, Battle-Cruiser Fleet, Rosyth (Vice-Admiral Sir David
Beatty):

YOU SHOULD CONCENTRATE TO EASTWARD OF LONG FORTIES
READY FOR EVENTUALITIES.[4]

Commander-in-Chief to:

Senior Officer, Battle-Cruiser Fleet, Rosyth.
Senior Officer, 5th Battle Squadron, in company (Rear-Admiral Evan-
Thomas):

URGENT. PRIORITY.

Admiralty telegram.

Available vessels Battle-Cruiser Fleet, Fifth Battle Squadron and T.B.D*s*
proceed to approximate position Lat. 56° 40′ N., Long. 5° 0′ E.

Desirable to economise on T.B.D*s*' fuel.

Presume you will be there about 2 p.m. tomorrow 31st. I shall be in
about Lat. 57° 45′ N., Long. 4° 15′ E. by 2 p.m. unless delayed by fog.

If no news by 2 p.m. stand towards me to get in visual touch.[4]

Commander-in-Chief to:

Senior Officer, 2nd Battle Squadron, Invergordon (Vice-Admiral Sir
Thomas Jerram):

Leave as soon as ready.

Meet me 2 p.m. tomorrow 31st, Lat. 57° 45′ N., Long. 4° 15′ E.

Several enemy submarines known to be in North Sea.[4]

Narrative of Commander The Hon. Barry Bingham,
Captain of the destroyer *Nestor*:

Things seemed as peaceful as could be on the afternoon of Tuesday, May
30th, when Maurice Bethell and I went ashore for a round of golf at Brunts-
field near Edinburgh. After a thoroughly enjoyable game over this course,
whose delightful inland surroundings reflected all the charm of early summer,
we adjourned for tea to "Rospletha"—the little house I had rented on the

side of the links—and then found our way down to Queensferry Pier at the regulation hour of 6 p.m., in order to catch the routine boat.

While we stood waiting on the pier amid a throng of fellow-officers, all eyes were suddenly drawn in the direction of the *Lion*, from whose masthead there floated a string of flags with their message to all ships—"Raise steam for 22 knots and bank fires at half an hour's notice."[6]

The Grand Fleet on this date was distributed between Scapa Flow, Invergordon and Rosyth.

The major portion was with the Commander-in-Chief at Scapa Flow, including the 1st and 4th Battle Squadrons and 3rd Battle-Cruiser Squadron, with the 2nd Cruiser Squadron (only organised that day from the 2nd and 7th Cruiser Squadrons) and the 4th Light Cruiser Squadron. With them were the 4th Destroyer Flotilla, part of the 11th Flotilla and the 12th Flotilla.

At Invergordon were the 2nd Battle Squadron, the 1st Cruiser Squadron, and part of the 11th Flotilla.

Vice-Admiral Sir David Beatty was at Rosyth with the *Lion* and 1st and 2nd Battle-Cruiser Squadrons. The 5th Battle Squadron was there, too, with the 1st, 2nd and 3rd Light Cruiser Squadrons and the 1st Flotilla, the 13th Flotilla, part of the 9th Flotilla and part of the 10th Flotilla; also the seaplane carrier *Engadine*.[29]

At Scapa, Invergordon and Rosyth, the single flag hoist necessary to bring the ships to the ready ran up to the yardarms of *Iron Duke*, *King George V* and *Lion* and were repeated round the fleets. A stream of boats scurried from ships to shore and back again, picking up recalled liberty men hastily rounded up by the shore patrols, while from the funnels of a hundred ships billowed the black smoke that showed they were urgently raising steam.[28]

At the three bases, streams of bunting climbed from the signal-bridges and searchlights blinked from ship to ship as the squadrons prepared for sea:

Scapa: C-in-C to Battle Fleet:
        Prepare to leave Scapa.
Rosyth: S.O. Battle-Cruiser Fleet to 1st and 2nd Battle-Cruiser Squadrons,
    5th Battle Squadron, 1st, 9th and 13th Destroyer Flotillas:
        Raise steam for 22 knots and report when ready to proceed.
Invergordon: S.O. 2nd Battle Squadron to 2nd Battle Squadron:

Prepare to leave Cromarty. Raise steam for 18 knots and report when ready to proceed.

Scapa: C-in-C to Cruisers and Destroyers:
Raise steam for 20 knots.

C-in-C to Battle Fleet:
Raise steam for 19 knots.

Rosyth: S.O. Battle-Cruiser Fleet to all squadrons in company:
Commanders of squadrons to report time at which their squadrons will be ready to proceed.

Squadrons to S.O. Battle-Cruiser Fleet:
5th Battle Squadron ready to proceed 9.40 p.m.
1st Battle-Cruiser Squadron 8.45 p.m.
2nd Battle-Cruiser Squadron 9 p.m.
1st Light Cruiser Squadron 8.23 p.m.
2nd Light Cruiser Squadron 9 p.m.
3rd Light Cruiser Squadron 8 p.m.
9th Destroyer Flotilla 8.30 p.m.
1st Destroyer Flotilla 9 p.m.
Engadine 9.45 p.m.

Scapa: C-in-C to 3rd Battle-Cruiser Squadron:
Raise steam for 22 knots. At what time will 3rd B.C.S. be ready to sail?

3rd Battle-Cruiser Squadron to C-in-C:
8.15 p.m.

Invergordon: Erin to S.O. 2nd Battle Squadron:
I should like to fill up with coal if possible as amount short, about 100 tons, makes it rather awkward for centre boiler room.

S.O. 2nd Battle Squadron to *Erin*:
Collier has been ordered.

London: Admiralty to S.O*s* commanding East Coast, Lowestoft, Harwich, Nore:
Weather permitting, aircraft should scout to seawards at daylight tomorrow.

Scapa: C-in-C to S.O. 7th Cruiser Squadron
S.O. 4th Light Cruiser Squadron:
Will cruisers and 4th L.C.S. be ready to leave at 9.30 p.m.?

S.O*s*. 7th C.S. and 4th L.C.S. to C-in-C:
> Yes.

S.O. 4th Battle Squadron to C-in-C:
> 4th Battle Squadron ready to proceed 9.45 p.m.

S.O. 1st Battle Squadron to C-in-C:
> 1st Battle Squadron ready to proceed 9.45 p.m.

Rosyth: S.O. Battle-Cruiser Fleet to Battle-Cruisers, 5th Battle Squadron, *Engadine*:
> Unmoor, weigh western anchor. Shorten in to three shackles.

Scapa: C-in-C to Commodore, Flotillas:
> T.B.D*s* for Battle-Cruisers, Cruisers and 1st Battle Squadron to meet squadrons off Swona. Those for 4th Battle Squadron off Hoxa obstruction. Battle-Cruisers will be leaving at 9 p.m.

C-in-C to *Cyclops:*
> Gate to be opened at 9.30 for fleet leaving.

C-in-C to all squadrons and flotillas:
> Fleet will leave tonight by D.T.3 method, ships in close order. All squadrons pass East of Swona and North of Skerries, except 4th L.C.S. which is to go West of Swona and South of Skerries.
> Battle Fleet will alter to 90° at 1.30 a.m., cruisers conforming.

Rosyth: S.O. Battle-Cruiser Fleet to 2nd Battle-Cruiser Squadron, 5th Battle Squadron, 1st and 13th Flotillas:
> *Fearless* and 1st Flotilla are to precede 5th Battle Squadron out of harbour and screen them.
> Two of 9th Flotilla are to join 13th Flotilla.
> *Lydiard* and remainder of 9th Flotilla are to precede and screen 2nd Battle-Cruiser Squadron.

Invergordon: S.O. 2nd Battle Squadron to 2nd Battle Squadron:
> Proceed out of harbour in D.T.3 at 9.45 p.m., 18 knots.

S.O. 2nd Battle Squadron to *Erin*:
> Collier will not go alongside you.

S.O. 2nd Battle Squadron to Rear-Admiral, Invergordon:
> Request gate may be opened by 9.15 p.m.

Rosyth: S.O. Battle-Cruiser Fleet to all squadrons in company:
> Proceed out of harbour 9.30 p.m.

Scapa: C-in-C to all squadrons and flotillas:

> W/T organisation S. will be adopted 9.30 p.m. Ships addressed are to take W/T guard on the wavelength denoted from the time specified until further orders. *Revenge* Q. *St Vincent*, German interception. *Benbow* stand by S. *Superb* W. *Hercules* X.

Rosyth: S.O. Battle-Cruiser Fleet to all ships in company:

> Ships denoted to take W/T guard on wavelength denoted at 2115. *Lion* S.D.X. *Princess Royal* X. *Queen Mary* W. *Tiger* Q. *Indefatigable* U.

Scapa: S.O. 2nd Light Cruiser Squadron to 2nd L.C.S.:

> Weigh.

Rosyth: S.O. Battle-Cruiser Fleet to 5th Battle Squadron:

> Follow 1st B.C.S. out of harbour and take station five miles astern.

> S.O. 3rd Light Cruiser Squadron to *Yarmouth*:

> What is delay in weighing?

Yarmouth to S.O. 3rd L.C.S.:

> Anchor came up foul of port cable. I had to let go again.

Rosyth: S.O. Battle-Cruiser Fleet to all squadrons and flotillas:

> Pass N. of May Island, then steer 66°. Speed from outer gate 16 knots.

Scapa: S.O. 3rd Battle-Cruiser Squadron to 3rd B.C.S., *Chester, Canterbury*:

> 3rd B.C.S. is to be 10 miles ahead of cruiser line. *Chester* to be five miles astern of 3rd B.C.S. *Canterbury* five miles ahead of *Invincible*. Modified route B will be followed. Speed of advance 17 knots. Zigzag during early hours.

Rosyth: S.O. Battle-Cruiser Fleet to *Lydiard*:

> Slip and follow light cruisers.

Scapa: S.O. 4th Light Cruiser Squadron to 4th L.C.S.:

> Weigh.

Invergordon: S.O. 2nd Battle Squadron to 2nd B.S.:

> Weigh.

Rosyth: S.O. Battle-Cruiser Fleet to 1st Battle-Cruiser Squadron:

> Weigh.

Scapa: C-in-C to all squadrons and flotillas:

> Cease W/T communication except on sighting the Enemy or
> replying to the Admiral.

Rosyth: S.O. 5th Battle Squadron to 5th B.S.:

> Weigh.

Scapa: C-in-C to Admiralty:

> Priority.
> Fleet leaving 9.30 p.m. today, Tuesday.[4]

As though co-operating to preserve the movement's secrecy, the day was drawing to a close. Beacons flashed on against the twilight, marking Hoxa Sound. At 9.30 the first unit of light craft began to steam out from the channel into the darkness, leaving security and safety behind. Clouds hid the stars; the air was heavy and wet; the islands were looming, mysterious, opaque masses. In succession—each ship lifting anchor at the proper minute, division after division, squadron after squadron of dreadnoughts and cruisers, flotilla after flotilla of destroyers—the Grand Fleet got under way, passing out to sea, entering the swift currents of the Pentland Firth and turning eastward into the open swell. The ships were darkened; each saw her neighbour only as a dark, indistinct silhouette against the night. The men on the bridges stood stolidly at their duties; the crews at guns and look-out stations were suddenly tense and sober at the return to danger and warfare. Inside the ships, in another world of bright electric light and intense heat, the turbines hummed with steady drone, and the stokers' shovels rasped as they fed coal into the boiler-fires.

In the three groups from Scapa Flow, Cromarty and Rosyth, the total British Grand Fleet was composed of 28 battleships, 9 battle-cruisers, 8 armoured cruisers, 26 light cruisers, 5 flotilla-leaders, 73 destroyers, 1 seaplane-carrier and 1 special minelayer—all told, 151 ships of war. Large and small, they carried more than 1,700 guns. By 10.30 p.m., May 30, 1916, they were all at sea, moving eastward towards a rendezvous about eighty miles off the Skagerrak.[22]

"Valhalla in the Gotterdämmerung."

Narrative of Commander Georg von Hase,
First Gunnery Officer of the German battle-cruiser *Derfflinger:*

On 31st May 1916, the battle-cruisers weighed anchor at 3 a.m. There were the *Lützow* (flagship of the Officer Commanding the reconnaissance squadron, Vice-Admiral Hipper), *Derfflinger*, *Seydlitz*, *Moltke*, and *Von der Tann*. We had spent the night in the Schillig Roads, off the entrance to the Jadebusen.

It was a beautiful, clear night which soon gave place to a splendid morning. The sun rose magnificently, covered the sea with its golden rays and soon showed us the picture of the whole High Seas Fleet. Far ahead of us steamed the small cruisers in line ahead, surrounded by a cordon of destroyers steaming ceaselessly round the cruisers, on the look-out for enemy submarines, like dogs round a flock of sheep.

Then came the battle-cruisers. Five powerful ships with imposing names, the pride of the fleet. The battle-cruisers, too, were surrounded by a cordon of destroyers which circled round us like a swarm of excited insects.

Far astern the clear weather enabled us to see the main fleet, our ships of the line. These numbered twenty-two, a proud armada. They were led by the 3rd Squadron, our most modern ships, with the flagship, the *König*, ahead, then the Fleet-Flagship, the *Friedrich der Grosse*, flying the flag of the Commander-in-Chief, Admiral Scheer. Then the 1st Squadron, the ships of the *Heligoland* and *Nassau* class, and finally the 2nd Squadron, the obsolescent battleships of the *Deutschland* class, including my old ship the *Hessen*, in which I had for five years directed firing-practice as gunnery officer.

The ships of the line were surrounded by light cruisers, which served as a screen for both flanks of the fleet. In addition there was, of course, the usual swarm of destroyers scouting for submarines and mines.

We steered west of Heligoland and the Amrum Bank on a northerly course. One half of the gun-crews were manning the guns, the other half were sleeping in their hammocks slung near the guns or near their respective action stations.

After enjoying the sunrise I lay down again for another couple of hours' sleep, after which I appeared, shaved, washed and rested, for breakfast in the mess. Most of the officers had to forego the luxury of a careful toilette, as they couldn't get to their cabins between decks owing to the fact that all the hatches had been battened down and watertight doors closed.

Nearly everyone was agreed that this time there would be an action, but no one spoke of anything more important than an action involving the lighter fighting forces or the older armoured cruisers. No one thought of the possibility that the whole English fleet could be only a few hours away from us.[25]

Hipper's period of leave had entirely restored his health and strength. He was the Hipper of old, the lover of action, swift in decision, but the pleasantest of superiors to his staff on the bridge and always kind-hearted, even when some particular occurrence drew a sharp word.

That morning he had been saying he was certain the enemy would be encountered. They would be at it hammer and tongs by the afternoon. His staff were astounded. Their barometer of hope was not so high. Hipper stuck to his prophecy and even went on to express the view that there would be heavy losses of human life when they really got down to grips with the British—he always had a warm corner for the bluejacket—and then consoled himself with the reflection that "it was all in God's hands".[35]

At 5.37 in the morning a message reached Scheer on the bridge of the *Friedrich der Grosse*. One of his submarines had come to the surface three hundred miles away to report by wireless that she had sighted two British dreadnoughts, two cruisers, and several destroyers 60 miles east of the Firth of Forth, on a south-easterly course.

A few minutes later a message from a second submarine came in, reporting eight British battleships, with various light cruisers and destroyers, 60 miles east of Peterhead.

At the same time the German wireless and decoding station at Neumunster reported that intercepted British wireless despatches indicated that

two British dreadnoughts, or groups of dreadnoughts, had left Scapa Flow.

Scapa Flow—Cromarty—Firth of Forth . . . the messages contained the clue to the entire British movement, but Scheer was unable to piece their scanty information into the full picture which they signified. Jellicoe, he decided, was still at Scapa Flow.

The German admiral went on to the northward, passed through the German minefields, and emerged into the open North Sea in ignorance of the fact that, as the fleets were steaming, a freak of destiny would bring them into identical waters late in the afternoon.[22]

The poet Gorch Fock, sailing in the German cruiser *Wiesbaden*:

A world power rushes out for its race with death, a mighty fleet. Here we are only beaters, and the giant grey torpedo-boats are only hounds for great hunters such as a *Lützow*, a *Seydlitz* or a *Derfflinger*! Beware, John Bull, beware! German wrath, the fierce, smiling anger of a Siegfried at Saxon perfidy, is about to break over you.

How the ship trembles! As far as the eye can reach there are German ships of war, tearing, racing, wrathful hunters and hounds! Ever bluer is the sea, ever higher rise the mounting waves, ever whiter is the foam from our bows. How our wake flashes behind us! All the old gods have come back to fight with us. Valhalla in the Gotterdämmerung.[17]

"There seems to be something wrong with our bloody ships today."

A chance encounter between the light forces of Beatty and Hipper brings the British and German battle-cruisers into contact. They turn southward at high speed on parallel courses, and a fierce engagement develops.

Owing to a misunderstanding, the 5th Battle Squadron of four powerful battleships, attached to Beatty's battle-cruisers, is temporarily left astern. While they are striving to catch up two British battle-cruisers are sunk.

Beatty orders his destroyers to attack; and during the ensuing action the situation is suddenly transformed by the appearance of Scheer, steaming northward towards the scene of the battle with the whole strength of the High Seas Fleet.

As the long hours of the middle watch crept on towards dawn of May 31st, even in the British fleet flagship there was no indication that this was to be anything but yet another abortive sweep.

Through the forenoon the situation remained the same and, with the fuel consumption of his destroyers in mind, Jellicoe steamed at the economical pace of fifteen knots, his advance further slowed by zigzagging and, from time to time, delays while ships and fishing vessels were examined.

Meanwhile, some sixty-five miles to the southward, Beatty's force was approaching the eastward limit set for his advance where, according to his orders, he was to turn north and make for a junction with Jellicoe's battle squadrons. As far as the eye could see there was no wisp of smoke or sign of ships except from his cruiser scouting line spread across ahead of him in pairs, the centre of the screen eight miles away to the E.S.E.

The battle-cruisers were in two columns, each in line ahead. Five miles astern were the four ships of the Fifth Battle Squadron and around the whole formation of heavy ships were the weaving, bustling, black shapes of the destroyer screen.

At 2 p.m. the time had come for Beatty to prepare the squadron for the turn to the northward, and a general signal to that effect was hoisted in the *Lion*. Punctually at 2.15 the signal to turn was hauled down and the whole force swung round on to a northerly course.

At this moment the incalculable element of chance intervened.[28]

Narrative of the Wireless Officer of the cruiser *Galatea* (Flagship of the 1st Light Cruiser Squadron, with Beatty's battle-cruisers):

Galatea, on the wing, was late in receiving the signal, and about 2.15 was only just about to turn when a merchant ship (the Danish tramp *N.J. Fiord*) was sighted ahead, which appeared to be stopped and blowing off steam. So the Commodore held on his course for a few minutes to have a look at her. On approaching her a little closer a destroyer, which had not at first been seen, was observed to leave her side, and at once was noted by her stump foremast and tall mainmast to be unmistakably a Hun. Action stations were at once sounded off.

I was aft on the quarter-deck quietly basking in the sun, and on hearing the bugle was in little hurry as I had heard that we were going to action stations for drill purposes sometime during the afternoon. So I strolled forward to my station—a little home-made Wireless Office on the foc'sle, more like a rabbit hutch than a W/T office, where I coded and decoded signals. But just as I went up the ladder on to the foc'sle I was deafened by the report of the foc'sle 6-inch gun firing, and was almost blown down the ladder again by its blast.

I nipped into my little W/T rabbit hutch quicker than it takes to tell, and as I entered there rattled down the communication tube from the upper bridge, in a small brass case, the first enemy report of the Battle of Jutland—[16]

2.20 P.M.

Galatea to ships in company:

Enemy in sight.

2.20 P.M.

Galatea to Beatty:

Urgent. Two cruisers, probably hostile, in sight bearing E.S.E., course unknown. My position Lat. 56° 48′ N., Long. 5° 21′ E.[4]

2 GERMAN
DESTROYERS

N.J.Fiord P

N

GALATEA

2nd BATTLE
CRUISER SQDN

1st BATTLE-CRUISER
SQDN

CRUISERS

5th BATTLE SQDN

On receiving this report, Beatty decided to set a course to get between the enemy and his base, and accordingly, at 2.32 p.m. he turned the Battle-Cruiser Fleet to S.S.E.—[3]

2.32 P.M.
Beatty to Battle-Cruiser Fleet:
> Alter course leading ships together the rest in succession to S.S.E.[4]

The turning signal, made by flags, was not seen by the *Barham* (flagship of the Fifth Battle Squadron) owing to the heavy smoke belched forth by the battle-cruisers in pressing on steam. Beatty was unaware that Evan-Thomas had neither received the *Galatea's* enemy report nor the turning signal.

At 2.38 p.m. Evan-Thomas, realising the true situation, also turned to S.S.E. This was six minutes after Beatty, and since the two squadrons had meanwhile been steaming in opposite directions, the gap between them had widened to nearly ten miles.[3]

2.38 P.M.
Beatty to Battle-Cruiser Fleet:
> Hands are to be stationed at action stations.[4]

The Executive Officer of the battleship *Warspite* (third ship of the 5th Battle Squadron:
> 2.40 p.m. Message from the Captain by his messenger "to get the hands up at once". I at once sounded off "action" and passed the word round to everybody that we were in for the real thing. Went all round mess decks; wetted decks, put all tables and stools on the deck, and lit all "Action Candles". Saw all doors and everything closed, and went up on deck. There was nothing in sight except our own ships, but we were steaming hard. Hoisted Battle Ensigns and Union Jack at after struts and masthead.[16]

Petty-Officer E. Francis, in the battle-cruiser *Queen Mary*:
> I heard in the distance a bugle sound of "Action". I was so surprised that I could hardly believe my ears, but the rush of feet by the door forced it upon me.

I took the first hatchway up, and came up to the foremost 4-inch battery, starboard side, and raced for "X" turret.

When I got inside everyone was there. I yelled out "Turret's crew, number." They were correct from top to bottom, and I reported to the Lieutenant of the Turret. He said, "Test loading gear, but for goodness' sake don't let them go too rash." The loading gear and machinery were tested, and immediately afterwards came the order to load all cages.[16]

An officer of the battle-cruiser *Princess Royal*:

Communications and instruments were quickly tested. The various parties were mustered at their stations; gas masks, goggles, and life-saving belts produced, and all other final preparations for action made. Splinter mats, fire hoses, boxes of sand, stretchers, medical instruments and drugs, leak-stopping gear, shoring-up spars, spare electrical gear, spare hydraulic gear, engineers' spare gear—all these were got ready in a few minutes as nearly everything was kept permanently ready for action when at sea.[16]

A midshipman of the battleship *Malaya* (rear ship of the 5th Battle Squadron):

I remember being chased off the bridge by the Captain and proceeding to my action station in the torpedo control tower, and on getting there discovering that some of the control instruments were in the Torpedo Control Officer's cabin, so I was sent down to get them. All doors and hatches had been shut when action was sounded off, so I had to open a door to get into the cabin flat. The Chief Carpenter was the Officer responsible for seeing these doors were shut, and unfortunately I met him on the way back, and in spite of all my pleadings had to leave him still convinced that it was his bounden duty to report me to the Commander for the grave offence of opening a water-tight door without permission. I spent the rest of the time until we opened fire wondering how much the punishment would be, and what was the best way of minimising the pain thereof.[16]

Galatea's Wireless Officer:

The first enemy report was shortly followed by several others, as first of all two German light cruisers with several more destroyers were sighted, and then more light cruisers and more destroyers.

I was busy coding the several signals which were sent down to me, but could hear in between the firing of our guns the long, drawn out whine of the enemy shells passing overhead, and a couple of crashes to port as two shells fell in the water just beyond us.

Very soon afterwards there was a terrific bump just outside the little W/T room in which I was sitting, and a shell hit us below the bridge, but fortunately for all of us on the foc'sle and bridge, it did not explode. An R.N.R. seaman saw it there a couple of minutes later, and thinking—goodness knows why—that it was one of our shells that had fallen down, tried to pick it up.

"Crikey, the blighter's hot," he yelled, and let go of it.[16]

N.J. Fiord, eager to escape from these dangerous waters and the menace of gunfire, made off from the scene with all the power of her ancient engine.

She had been responsible for contact between outlying units of Beatty's and Hipper's forces, and the contact was to lead to the Battle of Jutland—to the slaughter of thousands of men, the destruction of material and ships, the struggle for sea-power, the waste of nations' wealth, the clash of fleets created for the very deadly role they were to play today. Thus, events trivial in themselves become milestones of history, and thus, on May 31, 1916, the chance presence of a small neutral steamer in a certain portion of the North Sea, set the mighty forces of war into motion.[22]

2.39 P.M.
Galatea to Beatty:
>Urgent. Have sighted large amount of smoke as though from a fleet bearing E.N.E.[4]

Beatty's report:
From *Galatea*'s reports it was evident that the enemy force was considerable, and not merely an isolated unit of light cruisers, so at 2.45 p.m. I ordered *Engadine* to send up a seaplane—[4]

2.47 P.M.
Beatty to *Engadine*:
>Send up seaplanes to scout N.N.E. Am sending two destroyers to you.[4]

At 3.8 p.m. a two-seater Short seaplane with a 225 h.p. Sunbeam engine flew off the water with Assistant Paymaster G. S. Trewin as Observer and Flight-Lieutenant F. J. Rutland as Pilot. "The picture from the air," says one of these officers, "of the battle-cruisers and the 5th Battle Squadron with their attendant light cruiser screen and destroyers, all rushing forward in what may be termed an orderly helter-skelter to cut off the enemy, is a picture that can never be forgotten."[15]

Report of Flight-Lieutenant Rutland:
I was hoisted out at 3.7 p.m. and was off the water at 3.8 p.m.

I steered N 10, and after about ten minutes sighted the enemy. Clouds were at 1,000 to 1,200 feet, with patches at 900 feet. This necessitated flying very low.

On sighting the enemy it was very hard to tell what they were, and so I had to close to within a mile and a half at 1,000 feet.

The enemy's anti-aircraft firing was fairly good; the shock of exploding shrapnel could be felt, the explosions taking place about 200 feet away on one side, in front and astern.

When the Observer had counted and got the dispositions of the enemy and was making his W/T report, I steered to about 3 miles, keeping the enemy well in sight.

At 3.45 p.m. a petrol pipe leading to the left carburettor broke, and my engine revolutions dropped from 1,000 to 800, and I was forced to descend.[16]

The observer had sighted three enemy cruisers and several destroyers. Her signals, however, never got past the *Engadine*; and the *Engadine* picked her up while the battle-cruisers passed swiftly on.[29]

Up till 3.20 each Admiral was still unaware of the other's presence, but at that time, Admiral Hipper, though still some fourteen miles away upon the *Lion's* starboard bow, sighted two columns of British battle-cruisers steering towards him. So much less was the visibility to the eastward that it was not until about twelve minutes later that Admiral Beatty sighted the enemy's five battle-cruisers on his port bow.[11]

Sir John Jellicoe, with his deep professional seriousness and interest in modern naval technology, was not at all typical of those who dominated the

Royal Navy of 1916. Sir David Beatty was. Himself of the Anglo-Irish gentry, he had married the divorced daughter of Marshall Field, the American retail store millionaire. She had bought him a steam yacht, a house in the Leicestershire hunting country, and a Scottish grouse moor. . . . However, there were disadvantages, as Beatty discovered after his marriage, for his wife was an unstable neurotic who caused him extreme mental tortures.

Beatty himself was an able and intelligent officer, but his origins, his social and sporting obligations and his own brave but highly-strung temperament prevented him from becoming a coldly calculating professional like Jellicoe —or Hipper.

To a certain kind of uncritical admirer, Beatty with his square thrusting jaw, the cap worn at a slant, the dark hair worn long and thick, the thumbs rakishly stuck in the pockets of a monkey-jacket with six buttons instead of the regulation eight, made a more Nelsonian figure than the small, inscrutable Jellicoe. They did not observe the private unhappiness and uncertainty in that hollow pose; how more like those of an actor-manager than a sailor were his good looks.

Jellicoe and Beatty were destined each to fight their own separate battle at Jutland; and it was Beatty who fought first.[3]

von Hase, in *Derfflinger*:

A message from the Captain reached me in the fore-control: "Enemy battle-cruisers have been reported."

It was now clear that within a short time a life-and-death struggle would develop. For a moment there was a marked hush in the fore-control. I adjusted my periscope to its extreme power—fifteen diameters. Still there was no sign of the enemy.

Nevertheless, we could see a change. Our light cruisers and destroyers had turned about and were taking shelter behind the battle-cruisers. The horizon ahead of us grew clear of smoke, and we could now make out some English light cruisers which had also turned about.[25]

Executive Officer of *Warspite*:

Got orders to "load and train Red 20." Could not see anything at all, hazy and a lot of smoke about. We were steaming very hard. Wondered if our steering jackstaff would be shot away, as we had just fitted a new one. Everybody in the turret in very good spirits, and I asked G. if he had any cotton wool. He said he hadn't, and passed me a lump of cotton waste large enough to stop the ears of a donkey, which I chucked back at him; and almost at once we got the order to "stand by."[16]

von Hase, in *Derfflinger*:

Suddenly my periscope revealed some big ships. Black monsters. Six tall, broad-beamed giants steaming in two columns. Even at this great distance they looked powerful, massive. How menacing they appeared, magnified fifteen times. I could now recognise them as the six most modern enemy battle-cruisers. Six battle-cruisers opposed to our five.

The dark grey giants approached like fate itself.[25]

In *Warspite*:

Found we were turning fast to starboard, and as we came round I saw five enemy battle-cruisers on port bow, about Red 40. They were steaming the same way as we were and going very hard. A mass of black smoke, and I could only see their masts and the tops of their funnels above the horizon, and stern waves showing up white and very high.[16]

An officer of *Princess Royal*:

5 German battle-cruisers faintly distinguishable a very long distance away, accompanied by some torpedo craft. First of all their smoke, and later the outline of their masts, funnels, and the upper parts of their hulls.[16]

von Hase:

Our flagship *Lützow*, immediately astern of which we were following as second in line, swung round on a southerly course. The enemy also altered to a southerly converging course. And so both lines steamed south at full speed, coming continually nearer together.

Admiral Hipper's intention was clear: he meant to engage the enemy battle-cruisers and draw them on to our main fleet.

The log-keeper entered my orders:

"Ship turning to starboard. . . . Normal direction for starboard fire. 17,000! 16,500! Heavy guns, armour-piercing shell. Direction on second battle-cruiser from the right, 102 degrees. Deflection 91 left. Rate 100 minus. 16,400! . . ."

Still no permission to open fire from the flagship.[25]

An officer of the battle-cruiser *New Zealand*:

I had great difficulty in convincing myself that the Huns were in sight at last, it was so like battle exercise. It all seemed very cold-blooded and mechanical, no chance here of seeing red, merely a case of cool scientific calculation and deliberate gunfire. Everyone seemed cool enough in the control position, all sitting quietly at their instruments waiting for the fight to commence.[16]

On the Admiral's bridge of the *Lützow* Hipper stood, his trim beard thrust out aggressively, the inveterate cigar clamped between his teeth, a figure of inspiring confidence to those around him. All he wanted was to get into range as quickly as possible for he knew his ships could be outranged by the 13·5-inch guns of the enemy.[28]

At 3.45 p.m. Beatty, who was rapidly closing Hipper, formed line of battle on a line bearing north-west from the *Lion*, in the order *Lion, Princess Royal, Queen Mary, Tiger, New Zealand,* and *Indefatigable*. Meanwhile the Fifth Battle Squadron had shortened its distance to about seven miles to the north-west and were pressing on at full speed.[8]

von Hase:

The six ships, which had been proceeding in two columns, formed line ahead. Like a herd of prehistoric monsters they closed on one another with slow movements, spectre-like, irresistible.

I identified our target as the *Princess Royal*, a sister-ship of the *Queen Mary*.

All was ready to open fire, the tension increased every second, but I could not yet give the first order to fire. I had to wait for the signal from the flagship.[25]

The Navigating Officer of *New Zealand:*

Our Captain, John Green, was wearing the Maori rush kilt or war mat, called a piu-piu, which had been given to the ship by a Maori Chief in the

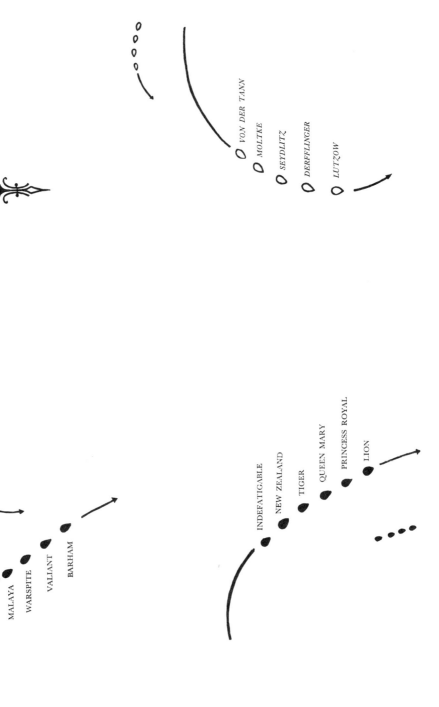

N

VON DER TANN
MOLTKE
SEYDLITZ
DERFFLINGER
LUTZOW

GALATEA

MALAYA
WARSPITE
VALIANT
BARHAM

INDEFATIGABLE
NEW ZEALAND
TIGER
QUEEN MARY
PRINCESS ROYAL
LION

ship's cruise round the world in 1913–14, with the injunction that it was always to be worn by the Captain of the *New Zealand* when in action.

It was made of strips of flax woven together at the top and was worn tied round the waist. The strips reached down to the knee and at intervals were dyed black, giving the appearance of a black and white kilt. Much faith was put in this mascot by the seamen, and word was passed round that the skipper was wearing the piu-piu all right.[16]

von Hase:

"15,000!"

As my last order rang out there was a dull roar. I looked ahead. The *Lützow* is firing her first salvo and immediately the signal "Open fire" is hoisted. In the same second I shout "Salvoes—Fire!" and the thunder of our first salvo crashes out.[25]

From the *Lion's* bridge the dim outline of the German ships could be seen, but no details could be picked out. They were in the order *Lützow, Derfflinger, Seydlitz, Moltke, Von der Tann*. At 3.48 p.m. the gun flashes of their first salvoes rippled down their line, stabbing the haze, and a few seconds later the reassuring roar of the *Lion's* first salvo rent the air.[8]

Having one ship more than his opponent, Beatty was able, while preserving the rule of keeping all the enemy under fire, to order the *Princess Royal*, his next astern, to concentrate with him on the *Lützow*, in which Admiral Hipper was leading. But the *Queen Mary*, which was third in the line, having apparently missed the signal for distribution of fire, took her opposite number, the *Seydlitz*, so that until she realised what was happening, the *Derfflinger*, which was second in the enemy's line, was left undisturbed for nearly ten minutes. In the rear half of our line a similar error occurred. The *Tiger*, the *Queen Mary's* next astern, appeared also to have missed the signal, so that she and the *New Zealand*, who had correctly taken the fourth ship, were both on the *Moltke*, while the *Indefatigable* and *Von der Tann* enjoyed an undisturbed duel.[11]

The Gunnery Officer of *Tiger*:

3.50 *Lion* opened fire, and we opened fire. Target 4th ship from right, range 18,500. Our first salvo missed for deflection, second salvo was over. The screen of destroyers on our engaged bow were causing great interference with their funnel smoke, and the enemy line was covered in cordite smoke from their guns firing. The smoke and flashes of the enemy salvoes when coinciding with our fall of shot made spotting very difficult.

3.52 the Germans were firing rapidly and getting our range. I saw splinters fly from our foc'sle past the gun control tower.[16]

An officer of *Tiger*:

The German shooting was very good. I remember watching the shells coming at us. They appeared just like big bluebottles flying straight towards you, each time going to hit you in the eye. Then they would fall, and the shell would either burst or else ricochet off the water and lollop away above and beyond you, turning over and over in the air.[16]

von Hase:

The Zeiss lenses of our periscopes were excellent. At the longest distances I could make out all details of the enemy ships, as, for instance, movements of the turrets and individual guns, which were lowered almost to the horizontal for loading.[25]

In the conning tower of *Princess Royal*:

They are getting very close. They have straddled us. No. 3 of the enemy line has been hit and is on fire. We have been hit forward. M. staggered into the conning tower badly burnt all over and reported a large number of his gun's crews killed or wounded.[16]

von Hase:

Each salvo fired by the enemy raised colossal splashes. Some of these columns of water were of a poisonous yellow-green tinge. The columns stood up for quite five to ten seconds before they collapsed again.[25]

The Germans found the range very quickly. Four minutes after opening fire the *Lion* was hit twice. A minute afterwards the *Tiger* was also hit—[8]

Gunnery Officer of *Tiger*:

— "Q" and "X" turrets did not come to the "ready". I had felt the concussion from hits on our armour, though I did not know for some minutes that both these turrets had been penetrated. "X" turret came in again after missing two or three salvoes, though with only one gun except at long intervals. I increased the rate of fire as much as possible, firing double salvoes. We received several more hits—[16]

In the engine-room of *Tiger*:

—a heavy thud, followed by a deafening report immediately overhead, intimated that a heavy shell had penetrated the side armour and had burst inboard. The shell bursting in the ammunition passage killed a dozen men, cut through the fresh and salt water mains, and finally the base of the shell, in penetrating to the engine-room, severed the H.P. air pressure ring main. The engine-room was immediately filled with dense smoke. Gauges and telegraphs could only be examined by the aid of electric torches. To add to the difficulties, water from the severed mains poured through the damaged deck overhead, over the separators, and over the main steam pipes on to the platform, so that the men stationed there were subjected, as the ship rolled, to alternate cascades of cold and semi-boiling water.[16]

von Hase:

The first hit struck us just over the casemate. It pierced a door with a round glass window, behind which Boatswain's Mate Lorenzen had taken shelter to watch the battle. His curiosity was severely punished, the shot severing his head clean from his body.[25]

An officer of *Princess Royal*:

Just as we saw the red-black burst of one of our shells hitting on the leading enemy ship, we noticed the *Lion* ahead of us hit amidships.[16]

The shell had struck "Q" turret, entered the gun-house and burst over the left gun. Nearly all the guns' crews were killed and all the men in the working chamber killed or wounded. Major Harvey, R.M.L.I., the officer of the turret, was severely wounded, but was able to pass the word down to close the magazine doors and flood magazines, a precaution which saved the ship and won him a V.C. in death.

45

A fire started in the wreckage of the turret, and a charge slid back from the gun and fell into the well. The fire caught it and spread to the charges in the gun-cages, then down the main trunk to the charges there. It gathered in a great flash of flame which passed right up and down and through the turret, penetrating up the escape trunk into the switchboard compartment and killing instantly all there. Their bodies and clothes were not burnt, and where they had screened their faces with their hands, their skin was not even singed. It reached the doors of the magazines, but they were closed.[29]

On the bridge of *Lion*:

A bloodstained sergeant of Marines appeared on the admiral's bridge. His clothes were burnt, and he seemed dazed. I asked him what was the matter: in a tired voice he replied, " 'Q' turret has gone, sir. All the crew are killed, and we have flooded the magazines."

I looked over the bridge. No further confirmation was necessary; the armoured roof of "Q" turret had been folded back like an open sardine tin, thick yellow smoke was rolling up in clouds from the gaping hole, and the guns were cocked up in the air. All this happened within a few yards of where Beatty was standing, and none of us on the bridge heard the detonation.[8]

As the two lines of great ships thundered along with belching, flaming guns, there appeared between them a vision of peaceful beauty in startling contrast to the savage scene. Lying becalmed, with all sails set, floated a barque, the crew whistling for a wind. Now as they looked on amazed, over their heads roared the shells, British and German, on their deadly murderous way through the calm summer air.[28]

In "X" turret of *Queen Mary*:

The gun's crew were absolutely perfect, inclined to be a little swift in loading, but I gave them a yell and pointed out to them that I wanted a steady stride, and after that everything went like clockwork.

My No. 3 said "Can you see what we're up against?" As soon as my gun had fired I had a quick look through the periscope, and it seemed to me there were hundreds of masts and funnels. I dropped back into my seat and while loading was being completed again I told them there were a few battle-cruisers, not wishing to put a damper on them in any way; not that I think it would have done so.[16]

Navigating Officer of *New Zealand*:
   The Admiral's Secretary came across to the Torpedo Officer and drew his attention to the *Indefatigable*. He crossed at once to the starboard side and laid his glasses on her. Whilst he was looking at her she was hit by two shells, one on the foc'sle and one on the fore turret. Both shells appeared to explode on impact. There was then an interval of about 30 seconds, during which there was absolutely no sign of fire or flame or smoke. At the end of the interval the ship completely blew up. The main explosion started with sheets of flame, followed immediately afterwards by a dense, dark smoke, which obscured the ship from view. All sorts of stuff was blown high into the air, a 50-foot steam picket boat being blown up about 200 feet.[16]

von Hase:
   The sound of what must have been a terrific explosion was completely drowned by the hellish din in our own ship and the bursting of the shells round us. The *Indefatigable* was engaged by our rearmost ship, the *Von der Tann*, and was sunk by the excellent shooting of that ship's First Gunnery Officer, Commander Mahrholz.[25]

Lieutenant W. S. Chalmers, in *Lion*:
   While out on the bridge I took the opportunity to have a look down our line. How magnificent our ships looked with their huge bow waves and flashing broadsides. Astern of the rear ship was a colossal pall of grey smoke. I gazed at this in amazement, and at the same time tumbled to the fact that there were only five battle-cruisers in our line. Where was the sixth? What ship was absent? Could it be that cloud of smoke? The unpleasant truth dawned upon me that the cloud of smoke was all that remained of the *Indefatigable*.[9]

In the gun control position of *New Zealand*:
   An Assistant Paymaster, who was keeping a record of the action immediately behind me, said "*Indefatigable*—hit"; he was going to say "sunk," but thought it might rattle the control party.[16]

A midshipman in *Malaya* (5th Battle Squadron):

Our enthusiasm knew no bounds when we passed a sunken ship with survivors swimming round her. We never dreamt that it was one of our battle-cruisers; but it was the *Indefatigable*, and over a thousand dead men lay in her wreck.[16]

A Medical Officer in the fore dressing station of *Princess Royal*:

Nothing impressed me more than the absolute absence of authentic news reaching us between decks. The only news was bad news, whispered to me by the Master-at-Arms, who was in my party, that the *Indefatigable* had been sunk.[16]

Hipper was almost rude when Commander Prentzel reported that the *Indefatigable* had been destroyed. It was only when he had seen for himself through the telescope that there were only five instead of six ships in the enemy's line that he felt real satisfaction. He rewarded Commander Prentzel for his piece of news with a grateful glance and then lit a fresh cigar.[35]

In *New Zealand*:

The loss of our next astern happened so suddenly that, almost before we realised she had gone, our attention was entirely absorbed in the fierce battle that was now progressing. The noise of our own salvoes, and the shrieking of the enemy's shells falling over or short, and throwing up great sheets of spray, left one with little time to think of anything except the work in hand.[16]

The 5th Battle Squadron had been coming up astern at full speed. They were still some seven or eight miles astern of the Battle-Cruiser Squadrons, but shortly after four o'clock their guns were beginning to range on the rear of the enemy's line.[29]

von Hase:

We saw that the enemy were being reinforced. Behind the battle-cruiser line appeared four big ships. We soon identified these as of the *Queen Elizabeth* class.* There had been much talk in our fleet of these ships. They were

* *Queen Elizabeth* herself was refitting at Rosyth at the time of Jutland. The other four ships of the class—*Barham, Valiant, Warspite* and *Malaya*—were all present as the 5th Battle Squadron.

48

ships of the line with the colossal armament of eight 15-inch guns, 28,000 tons displacement, and a speed of twenty-five knots. They fired a shell more than twice as heavy as ours. They engaged at portentous ranges.[25]

In *Warspite*:

Opened fire on No. 5. Spotting frightfully hard, and we were all short. Blast from "A" turret was awfully bad, and blew salt water and dust into my eyes, which watered like blazes. I saw several of their salvoes splash short of us; they made the dickens of a noise.[16]

A Midshipman of *Malaya*:

We heard the other ships of our own squadron open fire, each salvo helped on its way by a cheer. In our torpedo control tower we were so interested in what was going on that when *Malaya* herself opened fire the blast from "X" turret's guns, which were only a few feet away from us, sat us down with a "whump," and the range-taker came down from his seat with a crash.[16]

The end ships of the German line were thus exposed to a regular hail of fifteen-inch projectiles, *Von der Tann* being hit almost immediately.[21]

Beatty's report:

From 4.15 p.m. to 4.43 p.m. the conflict between the opposing battle-cruisers was of a fierce and resolute character. The 5th Battle Squadron was engaging the enemy's rear ships, unfortunately at very long range. At 4.18 p.m. the 3rd enemy ship was seen to be on fire—[4]

P.O. Francis in *Queen Mary*:

—the Transmitting Station reported that the third ship of the German line was dropping out. The shout they gave was good to hear. I felt the turret training a bit faster than she had been, and surmised we must have shifted on to the fourth ship.[16]

Gunnery Officer of *Tiger*:

I thought we were doing well. The enemy fire had slackened as far as we were concerned, but the smoke and gun-flashes still made spotting difficult.[16]

The British shells struck with terrific impact, but in many cases broke up as they did so, spending their force upon the armour.[22]

Hipper:
It was nothing but the poor quality of the British bursting charges that saved us from disaster.[36]

von Hase:
The *Queen Mary* had selected the *Derfflinger* as her target. I had to admit that the enemy were shooting superbly. I was trying to get in two salvoes to the enemy's one. Several times I was unable to attain this, as the enemy was firing with fabulous rapidity. But the poor *Queen Mary* was having a bad time. In addition to the *Derfflinger* she was being engaged by the *Seydlitz* and the gunnery officer of the *Seydlitz*, Lieutenant-Commander Foerster, was our crack gunnery expert.[25]

Derfflinger and *Seydlitz* began hitting *Queen Mary* with full intensity.

Valiant *Queen Mary*. Of all Britain's ships she was one of the most gallant, known throughout the fleet for her spirit and personality. She had dealt more blows than any other of Beatty's battle-cruisers today; she had struck *Seydlitz* thrice, causing heavy damage, and had so far escaped with little injury to herself. Now famous *Derfflinger*, untouched by a British shell, had come into play against her.[22]

An officer of *Tiger*:
The *Queen Mary* was next ahead of us, and I saw one salvo straddle her. Three shells out of four hit. The next salvo straddled her, and two more shells hit her. As they hit I saw a dull red glow amidships and then the ship seemed to open out like a puff ball, or one of those toadstool things when one squeezes it. Then there was another dull red glow somewhere forward, and the whole ship seemed to collapse inwards—[16]

—the column of smoke and flame that towered out of the exploding vessel was a thousand feet high; there was a swift vision of collapsing masts, of a hull rent in two; with the utmost difficulty *Tiger* and *New Zealand* sheered out to avoid the wreck, saw hundreds of objects catapulting into the air, saw the stern of the vessel rear up out of the water—[22]

Gunnery Officer of *Tiger*:
—we steamed on into the cloud. It was pitch black, we could not fire, so I used the opportunity to line up director*—[16]

—while the *Tiger* was passing through this dense smoke cloud, observers were amazed to see vast quantities of official forms and sheets of paper whirling about. These must have been suddenly released from an airlock in the stern of the stricken ship—[8]

—the *Tiger* passed her to port, the *New Zealand* to starboard. Her stern was high in the air with the propellers revolving. Men were crawling out of the after turret—[29]

P.O. Francis, one of the survivors of the *Queen Mary*:
—the ship had an awful list to port by this time, so much so that the men getting off the ladder went skidding down to port. . . .
. . . when I got to the ship's side there seemed to be quite a fair crowd. I called out to them, "Come on, you chaps, who's coming for a swim?" I clambered up over the slimy bilge keel and fell off into the water—[16]

A gunlayer in *Tiger*:
—the *Queen Mary* seemed to roll slowly to starboard, with a huge hole in her side. She listed again, the hole disappeared beneath the water, which rushed into her and turned her completely over—[34]

—suddenly the entire ship was rent by a terrific upheaval and disappeared. She had gone down, leaving only 17 survivors—[29]

von Hase:
—nothing but a thick, black cloud of smoke remained where the ship had been. At its base the smoke column only covered a small area, but it widened towards the summit and looked like a monstrous black pine.[25]

* i.e. he used the moment of black-out to check that the electrical receivers of the director firing system in each turret were all in step with the master instrument in the gun control position aloft.

Captain Chatfield, on the bridge of *Lion*:

Beatty turned to me and said, "There seems to be something wrong with our bloody ships today."[9]

And all the time the din of the regular salvoes had been uninterrupted; the loading crews had continued to thrust in shell and powder, the stokers had shovelled coal into the roaring furnaces, and both fleets had steamed through the geysers of water become so familiar that they were like a part of the seascape.[22]

Beatty, to Captain Destroyers, in *Champion*:

Attack the enemy with torpedoes.[4]

Bingham, in *Nestor*:

The *Champion* immediately repeated this order, adding that the *Nestor* and her division were to lead the attack. The attacking destroyers of the 13th, 10th and 9th Flotillas were as follows: *Nestor, Nomad, Nicator, Narborough, Pelican, Petard, Obdurate, Nerissa*, with *Moorsom* and *Morris* of the 10th Flotilla, *Turbulent* and *Termagent* of the 9th Flotilla.

I immediately hoisted the signal for full speed and ordered the destroyers to form a single line astern of me.[6]

Admiral Hipper saw the attack developing and launched his 9th Flotilla against it, supported later by the *Regensburg* and a portion of the 2nd Flotilla.[29]

With bow waves curling and creaming, their sterns tucked down into the white flurry of their stern waves, signal flags snapping in the wind of their wild progress, the sleek, slim little ships plunged into the arena . . . to meet in a wild melee in the centre with guns barking and torpedoes streaking in all directions—[28]

—a wild scene of groups of long low forms vomiting heavy trails of smoke and dashing hither and thither at thirty knots or more through the smother and splashes, and all in a rain of shell from the secondary armament of the German battle-cruisers, as well as from the *Regensburg* and the destroyers, with the heavy shell of the contending squadrons screaming overhead—[11]

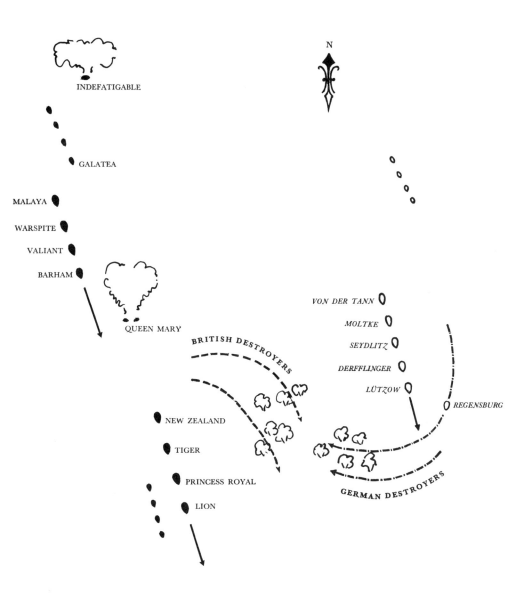

N

INDEFATIGABLE

GALATEA

MALAYA

WARSPITE

VALIANT

BARHAM

QUEEN MARY

BRITISH DESTROYERS

VON DER TANN

MOLTKE

SEYDLITZ

DERFFLINGER

LÜTZOW

REGENSBURG

NEW ZEALAND

TIGER

PRINCESS ROYAL

LION

GERMAN DESTROYERS

Bingham, in *Nestor*:

—*Nomad*, my immediate follower, was hit in the boiler-room and hauled out of line disabled. We in the *Nestor* got the range very quickly, and pumped in three or four salvoes from our 4-inch guns. Two German destroyers disappeared beneath the surface—[6]

in *Petard*:

— an accident happened to our second torpedo, for when fired it hung half out of the tube and broke at the joint between the head and the body . . . the business end, with all the explosive in it, was dangling over the side . . . the tube's crew gingerly trying to bear the head off with a boathook as it bumped against the side.[16]

The destroyer recall was flying, but the gallant *Nestor* was not to reach home. The *Regensburg*, appearing from behind the battle-cruisers, opened a heavy fire on her and succeeded in getting two shots into her boilers—[29]

Bingham, in *Nestor*:

—a huge cloud of steam was rising from the boiler-room, completely enshrouding the whole ship, and it was painfully apparent that our speed was dropping every second.

Seeing our plight the *Petard* gallantly offered a tow; but I had no hesitation in refusing an offer which would have meant the exposure of two ships to the danger that properly belonged to one.

Curiously enough, when our speed gave out, we found ourselves brought to a standstill at a spot only two miles west of *Nomad*, our only comrade in misfortune.[6]

As a result of these attacks the *Seydlitz* was hit by one torpedo, but although she took in a good deal of water she was able to hold her place in the line.[8]

While the destroyers had been engrossed in their own fast-moving, confused fight, a development of tremendous significance had suddenly arisen.

Ever since the opposing battle-cruisers had turned south, the British light cruiser line, left astern, had been straining every nerve to get ahead and take up their scouting positions. Of the three light cruiser squadrons composing the screen, the most southerly was the Second Light Cruiser Squadron under Commodore Goodenough, with his pendant in the *Southampton*. By 4.33 he had succeeded in getting two miles ahead of the *Lion* and, at that moment, to his astonished gaze, the topmasts of battleships to the south-eastwards hove into sight.

Claiming the utmost priority, the signal went out—[28]

4.38 P.M.
Southampton to Jellicoe and Beatty:
URGENT. PRIORITY.
Have sighted enemy battlefleet bearing approximately S.E., course of enemy N. My position Lat. 56° 34′ N., Long. 6° 20′ E.

Southampton to ships in company:
Battleships S.E. and reported by W/T Urgent Priority at 4.38 to Jellicoe and Beatty. Scheer coming north with the main body of the High Seas Fleet.[4]

What he had seen—and it was a sight no British ship had enjoyed since the war began—was the German High Seas Fleet deployed in battle order, line ahead. In the van, led by Rear-Admiral Behncke in the *König*, came the 3rd Squadron, seven of the "König" and "Kaiser" classes, the latest German Dreadnoughts. Following them were nine more Dreadnoughts—five "Helgolands," with twelve 12-inch guns and four "Nassaus" with twelve of 11-inch. In the rear was the 2nd Squadron—six pre-Dreadnoughts which, against his original intention, Admiral Scheer had brought with him at the urgent entreaty of its commander, Rear-Admiral Mauve. He himself, in the fleet flagship *Friedrich der Grosse*, was eighth ship in his selected post of command between the van and centre, and in company were five cruisers of the 4th Scouting Group and three and a half flotillas of destroyers, led by the light cruiser *Rostock*.[11]

If Beatty lacked the weapons with which to destroy this great dreadnought force, Jellicoe, only fifty miles away, was coming south at all speed with the entire weight of Britain's naval strength. If Beatty could decoy the German

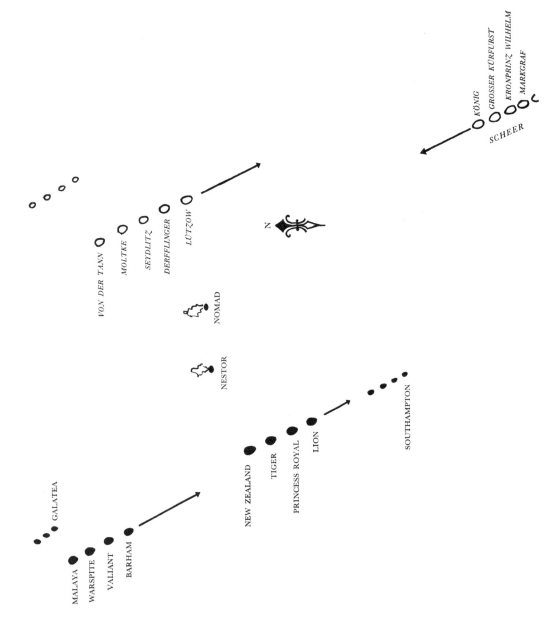

GALATEA

MALAYA

WARSPITE

VALIANT

BARHAM

NEW ZEALAND

TIGER

PRINCESS ROYAL

LION

SOUTHAMPTON

VON DER TANN

MOLTKE

SEYDLITZ

DERFFLINGER

LÜTZOW

N

NOMAD

NESTOR

KÖNIG

GROSSER KÜRFURST

KRONPRINZ WILHELM

MARKGRAF

SCHEER

fleet north, induce Scheer to hold his course for just another hour, then a general fleet engagement would take place compared with which the present action was mere preliminary.

He would then turn to the north and fight a retreating action, employing the identical tactics which Hipper had used to lure him south. But this time the retreat would be staged with sea-power itself as the stake.[22]

4.43 P.M.
Beatty to Battle-Cruiser Fleet:
    Alter course in succession 16 points to starboard.[4]

Bingham, in *Nestor*:
While lying helpless and broken down, we saw the opposing forces of battle-cruisers retracing their tracks to the N.W., fighting on parallel courses.

Fifteen minutes later my yeoman-of-signals reported: "German battle-ships on the horizon, shaping course in our direction." I was dumbfounded to see that it was in truth the main body of the German High Seas Fleet, steaming at top speed and following the wake of their own battle-cruisers.

Their course necessarily led them first past the *Nomad*, and in another ten minutes the slaughter began. They literally smothered the destroyer with salvoes. I shall never forget the sight, and mercifully it was a matter of a few minutes before the ship sank; at the time it seemed impossible that anyone on board could have survived.

Of what was in store for us there was now not the vestige of a doubt.[6]

From an affair of outposts, the situation had suddenly developed into what could well be the decisive action of the whole war. A drama of unparalleled grandeur and significance was about to unfold, though, to the Germans, the full implications were not yet clear. The most powerful figure on the stage was as yet unrevealed to them—Jellicoe, with his mighty array still pressing southwards, desperate to get into the battle and avid for every scrap of information.[25]

"Fleet Action is imminent."[13]

*Jellicoe, with the main British fleet, has been steaming down towards Beatty.
As the signals from Beatty's force tell him of its southward-moving action with
the German battle-cruisers, he increases to full speed. He then learns that the High
Seas Fleet has been sighted heading north towards him, and informs the
Admiralty that a fleet action is imminent.*

*Meanwhile Beatty turns north to lure the whole German fleet towards Jellicoe,
and the battle-cruiser action is renewed on a northerly course. During it Beatty is
severely mauled and momentarily disengages; but the 5th Battle Squadron, following
astern of him, and fighting the leading battleships of the High Seas Fleet as well as
Hipper's battle-cruisers, gives as good as it gets with its huge 15-inch guns.*

*Beatty, having got his damage under control, re-engages; and the two battle-
cruiser forces, followed by Scheer's battleships, steam swiftly north towards
Jellicoe—the Germans still being unaware of what lies ahead.*

Narrative of Captain F. C. Dreyer, captain of Jellicoe's flagship *Iron Duke*:

All the time, since 2.15 p.m., Jellicoe with the main body of the Grand
Fleet had been coming down from the north. At 2.20 the Battle Fleet was
steaming at 15 knots in six columns, each of four Dreadnought battleships,
the columns being disposed abeam. They were at short notice for full speed.[13]

Perhaps no sight more impressive has been seen at sea—not even Nelson's
two divisions standing in to destroy Villeneuve—than Jellicoe's 24 blue-grey
battleships in six columns abeam, the left-centre column led by *Iron Duke*
wearing Jellicoe's flag—a red St. George's cross on a white ground—their
bow waves curling higher and higher, and the thick, soft smoke streaming
away from their funnels into the still and sunlit afternoon. The characteristic
British silhouette of a battleship was a low straight hull, from which sprang

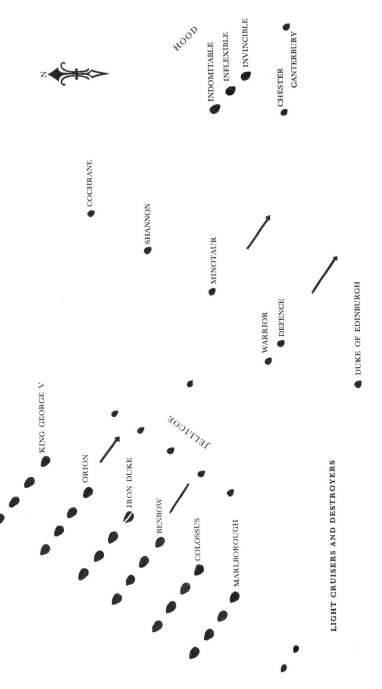

the verticals of narrow, closely placed un-raked funnels and tripod masts and fighting tops. *Neptune* and the two *Colossus* class ships were conspicuous for their ugliness, having what looked like a double-span railway bridge on the centre-line over the midships turrets.[3]

In front and on the flanks, thirty-nine destroyers acted as a submarine screen. Farther out, ten light cruisers were an outer screen, two on each flank and six up ahead, with the fast mine-layer *Abdiel* cruising free where she could easily steam off for special duty.

Out of sight, fifteen miles ahead, steamed the Grand Fleet vanguard, with the cruiser *Hampshire* and a destroyer stationed half-way between to relay signals. Seven armoured cruisers, each accompanied by a destroyer, were spread wide across the sea, so that each cruiser was just within sight of her neighbours. These were large vessels, the oldest of Jellicoe's ships, including *Black Prince, Duke of Edinburgh, Warrior* and *Defence; Minotaur, Shannon* and *Cochrane.*

Still farther ahead, at the tip of all, steamed the Third Battle-Cruiser Squadron, under Rear-Admiral Hood, who had the battle-cruisers *Invincible, Inflexible* and *Indomitable,* the new light cruisers *Chester* and *Canterbury,* and the destroyers *Shark, Acasta, Ophelia* and *Christopher.*[22]

Jellicoe was the modest son of a master of the merchant marine. His mind was a well-ordered filing system of detail, reflected by his small neat person, the tight mouth, and the watchful, calm brown eyes that looked out steadily past the prominent nose. His manner was cool, controlled and always polite. This self-containment rested on profound self-confidence. No officer had so profound and detailed an awareness of the Grand Fleet's strength; but also of its hidden and serious weaknesses. . . .

He was fifty-seven now, tough and fit. His staff found him off-duty a lively, approachable man, a generous host, but always careful and abstemious himself over food and drink. In harbour he worked a fifteen-hour day, wearing his gold-rimmed half-spectacles for reading. When the fleet was cruising, however, he was unable to relax his personal grip on it at all: "I never left my sea cabin, which was under the bridge, to go to the after part of the ship while the Fleet was at sea."[3]

On the eve of sailing, Admiral Scheer, in accordance with his usual practice, had transferred the call sign of his flagship to the naval centre at Wilhelmshaven, so that, although it was thought he had sailed that morning, our directional wireless up till noon could only indicate that the German battle fleet was still in the Jade. Thus, Admiral Jellicoe, who was informed of this by the Admiralty, had no special reason to expect the chance of an action.[11]

Jellicoe had taken in the *Galatea's* signals, and though there was nothing to lead him to expect anything more than an affair of cruisers, he ordered steam to be ready for full speed. A few minutes later he heard the *Galatea* reporting a large amount of smoke as though from a fleet bearing E.N.E. of her, and he then (2.43) ceased zigzagging and held on upon his normal course at 17 knots, increasing to 18 knots twelve minutes later.[11]

2.57 P.M.
Jellicoe to Battle Fleet:
Raise steam for full speed with all despatch.

3.00 P.M.
Jellicoe to Battle Fleet:
Assume complete readiness for action in every respect.

3.10 P.M.
Jellicoe to Cruisers:
Take up cruising disposition No. 1.
Centre of screen 16 miles from Battle Fleet.
Speed of advance 18 knots.
Assume complete readiness for action.

3.40 P.M.
Beatty to Jellicoe:
Urgent. Enemy Battle-Cruisers, five in number, bearing N.E. Destroyers, large number, bearing N.E., course unknown.

3.45 P.M.
Beatty to Jellicoe:
Urgent. Course of enemy S. 55 E. My position Lat. 56° 53′ N., Long. 5° 33′ E.

3.55 P.M.
Beatty to Jellicoe:
Urgent. Am engaging enemy.[4]

61

There was a sea-fight going on, but it was sweeping directly away from Jellicoe at the speed of battle-cruisers, sixty miles or more in front of him, and no power at which he could drive his ships could overtake it.

But the British Commander-in-Chief must support his battle-cruisers in every way possible. Every moment was taking them nearer to enemy waters. Jellicoe increased the Grand Fleet's speed to 20 knots, almost the utmost of which his dreadnoughts were capable—it was the greatest speed at which the fleet had ever steamed as a unit. He ordered the ships to steer clear of each other's wakes, so that they would make all possible progress through the water.

Simultaneously he ordered Admiral Hood to take the Third Battle-Cruiser Squadron on in advance at full speed, and, if possible, to join forces with Beatty.[22]

4.05 P.M.
> Jellicoe to Senior Officer, 3rd Battle-Cruiser Squadron (Admiral Hood):
> > Proceed immediately to support Battle-Cruiser Force. Position Lat. 56° 53′ N., Long. 5° 31′ E., course S. 55 E. at 3.50 p.m.[4]

Then for an anxious half-hour all was silence; not a word reached the Commander-in-Chief of how his colleague was faring. Of the 5th Battle Squadron he had heard nothing. He telegraphed to know if it was in company with the battle-cruisers—[11]

4.17 P.M.
> Jellicoe to Senior Officer, 5th Battle Squadron (Admiral Evan-Thomas):
> > Are you in company with S.O. Battle-Cruiser Fleet?

Reply
> Evan-Thomas to Jellicoe:
> > Yes, I am engaging enemy.

4.38 P.M.
> *Southampton* to Commander-in-Chief; to Senior Officer, Battle-Cruiser Fleet:
> > URGENT. PRIORITY.
> > Have sighted enemy battlefleet bearing approximately S.E., course of enemy N. My position Lat. 56° 34′ N., Long. 6° 20′ E.

4.45 P.M.
> Beatty to Jellicoe, via *Princess Royal*:*
>> URGENT. PRIORITY.
>> Have sighted enemy's battlefleet bearing S.E.
>> My position Lat. 56° 36′ N., Long. 6° 04′ E.

4.47 P.M.
> Jellicoe to Battle Fleet:
>> Enemy's battlefleet is coming North.

4.51 P.M.
> Jellicoe to Admiralty, London:
>> URGENT.
>> Fleet action is imminent.[4]

On receiving this signal the Admiralty alerted dockyards all along the East Coast:

Admiralty to C-in-C., Nore:
> Hold tugs in readiness.

Admiralty to C-in-C., Rosyth:
> Hold tugs in readiness.

Admiralty to Commodore, Harwich; Vice-Admiral, Dover:
> Hold tugs in readiness.

Admiralty to Senior Naval Officer, Jarrow
> Rear-Admiral, Invergordon
> Rear-Admiral, East Coast:
> Hold tugs in readiness.

Admiralty to Senior Naval Officer, Invergordon
> C-in-C., Rosyth
> Admiral Superintendent, Tyne:
> Fleet action imminent. All docks should be ready in case they are required for vessels of the fleet.[4]

At 4.43 the signal had streamed from *Lion's* battered yard-arm: "Alter course in succession 16 points (180 degrees) to starboard."

* The W/T aerials of Beatty's flagship *Lion* had been shot away. As he was turning north, he semaphored to *Princess Royal*, his next astern:
> Report enemy's battlefleet to Commander-in-Chief bearing S.E.

The flagship's helm went over as the flags were hauled down, and *Lion* described a massive curve through the sea, straightening out upon a north-westerly course. *Princess Royal, Tiger* and *New Zealand* followed her, making 25 knots—and the column steamed directly away from the approaching Scheer. Each ship checked her gunfire as she turned; the turrets trained round to the other beam, and as soon as the range was clear, the artillery duel against the German battle-cruisers was resumed. But events had taken place so rapidly that the British squadron had already come within gun-range of the High Seas Fleet, and Scheer's leading battleships had opened fire at the British battle-cruisers at the maximum elevation of their guns.

Between Beatty and the advancing German dreadnoughts the Second Light Cruiser Squadron was thrusting boldly forward in quest of information—[22]

Lieutenant Stephen King Hall, in *Southampton*, Flagship of the 2nd Light
Cruiser Squadron:

It was a strain steaming at twenty-five knots straight for this formidable line of battleships, with our own friends going fast away from us in the opposite direction.

As we got closer I counted sixteen or seventeen battleships with the four *König* class in the van.

Seconds became minutes and still they did not open fire, though every second I expected to see a sheet of flame ripple down their sides and a hail of shell fall around us. I can only account for this by the theory that, as they only saw us end on, they assumed we were a German light cruiser squadron that had been running away from the British battle-cruisers.[24]

4.48 P.M.
Southampton to Jellicoe and Beatty:

> URGENT. PRIORITY.
> Course of enemy's battlefleet, N., single line-ahead. Composition of van Kaiser class. Bearing of centre, E. Destroyers on both wings and ahead. Enemy's Battle-Cruisers joining Battlefleet from Northward.[4]

The Commodore saw that we could not get into a position for a torpedo attack and as we should be lucky if we got out of the desperately dangerous position we were then in, he gave the order for the turning signal, which had been flying for five minutes, to be hauled down.

Over went the helm, and our four ships slewed round, bringing our sterns to the enemy.

Crash! Bang! Whizzzz! And a salvo crumped down around us, the fragments whistling and sobbing overhead.[24]

Only one group of the British Battle-Cruiser Fleet was still coming down towards Scheer.

The Fifth Battle Squadron was still blazing out its heavy fire at the rear ships of Hipper's line.

At 4.52 Evan-Thomas passed by Beatty on an opposite course, and found his fire masked by the British battle-cruisers. Beatty tried to signal the course "North"—but Beatty's ships were surrounded by splashes rising from the concentrated fire of a dozen German vessels, and signal flags were indistinguishable. Evan-Thomas, astonished to see that his leader had only four ships left, held on to the south, thinking to take up the burden of the fight.

Then, a moment later, as he emerged from behind the last British battle-cruiser, he sighted the High Seas Fleet and grasped the situation. Almost immediately *Barham*, his flagship, was hit, and Evan-Thomas ordered an immediate turn after Beatty. As the helm went over, *Barham* was struck again. Amid a thunder of falling shells the Fifth Battle Squadron swung round to the north at 4.58, *Malaya*, the last ship, steering out of the line to avoid the ferocious German concentration. Hipper had likewise reversed his course and was now steering north in the van of the High Seas Fleet.[22]

In *Warspite*:

Very soon after the turn I suddenly saw on the starboard quarter the whole of the High Seas Fleet; at least I saw masts, funnels, and an endless ripple of orange flashes all down the line.[16]

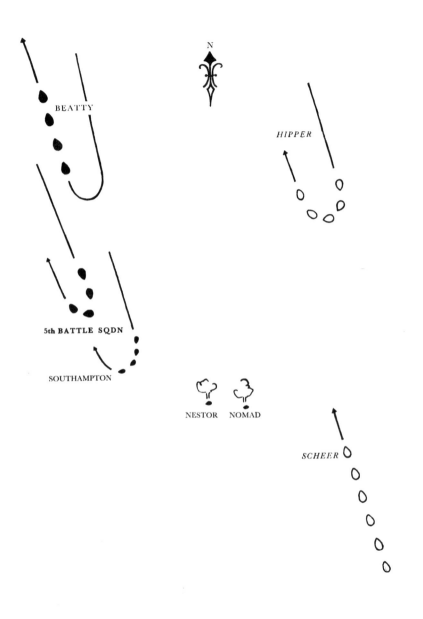

N

BEATTY

HIPPER

5th BATTLE SQDN

SOUTHAMPTON

NESTOR   NOMAD

SCHEER

A turret officer in *Malaya*:

When we had turned I saw that our battle-cruisers were already quite 7,000 or 8,000 yards ahead of us. I then realised that just the four of us of the 5th Battle Squadron alone would have to entertain the High Seas Fleet—four against perhaps twenty.[18]

King Hall in *Southampton*:

The fascination of watching these deadly and graceful splashes rising mysteriously from the smooth sea was enormous. To know that the next place where they would rise was being calculated by someone perched up in one of those distant masts, and that he was watching us through a pair of Zeiss binoculars—and I was watching his ship through a similar pair of Zeiss—was very interesting.[24]

Lion opened fire again on the leading enemy battle-cruiser (*Lützow*).

The other battle-cruisers also came into action again at a range of about 19,000 yards, except *New Zealand*, who was unable to get sufficient elevation on.

Princess Royal engaged the second ship in the line (*Derfflinger*) as *Lion's* smoke interfered with the view of the leading ship.

Tiger engaged the third ship (*Seydlitz*).[31]

Every British ship was being driven at top speed, firing her guns at the maximum rate, and receiving heavy enemy fire—every decision, every command, had been made and obeyed within seconds of time, in a furious changing panorama of battle. Within short minutes all the British force under Beatty had turned northward into a long, loose speeding column, belching smoke and turret action.[22]

In *Lion's* gun control top:

"Did you see that?"

"No."

"Down 400: close the rate 200."

"Can't."

"Make it one."

"Down 400 on the plot."
"Put it on and close 100."
"Rate 250 closing."
"Shoot!"
"Ship altering course to starboard, rate 200 closing."
"Stand by, splash."
"Up 200."[16]

An officer in *Lion*:

I was working on the chart in the Admiral's Plotting Room (immediately below the compass platform where Beatty was standing) when I felt the deck under my feet give a sudden heave. At the same moment the chart table, over which I was leaning, split in the centre and the windows fell in, exposing the chart and myself to the full blast of a head wind.

Before I could realise what had happened, the chart was torn in two, and the business half of it flew through the window. I last saw it fluttering over the sea like a frightened seagull.[9]

Lion's Gunnery Officer:

A quantity of wreckage is passed, on which two or three men are floating, and a destroyer is standing by near to it—apparently it is the remains of the *Queen Mary*.[16]

At this spot *Lion* seemed fated to follow *Queen Mary* to the bottom. The British flagship was afire in half a dozen places; shell fragments had riddled the salt-water mains and fire-hoses until it was almost impossible to get water to the flames, some of which roared up from powder-fires of terrific intensity. Since the beginning of the action *Lion* had been struck thirteen times by heavy shells. The main and gun-decks were littered with tangled wreckage; dead and wounded men lay everywhere through the batteries; electric lighting had been blown away—dim lanterns and flickering flames lit the smoky, stinking interiors.

Tiger, the third in line, had been hit seventeen times; *Princess Royal* had suffered heavily. Only *New Zealand*, ship with the talisman, had escaped virtually without injury. The battle-cruisers needed a breathing space.

Beatty turned north-west at 24 knots, to open the range and break off the action.[22]

Medical Officer of *Princess Royal*:
We dressed several cases, chiefly of burns occurring amongst members of the fire and repair parties . . . a gun-layer from the after turret had a foot nearly blown away . . . later on I amputated his leg . . . a Marine had been brought down bleeding seriously from a punctured wound of the face. . . I always remember him saying, "Lor' bless you, sir, they fires a lot, but they never 'urts each other."[16]

von Hase in *Derfflinger*:
We were burning to win fresh laurels. A feeling of exaltation reigned throughout the ship. The gun-barrels began to get very hot, the grey paint began to blister and turn brown and yellow.[25]

During this time the ships of the Fifth Battle Squadron were under heavy fire, as many as six salvoes per minute falling round *Malaya* at one period, several of which hit—

5.00 P.M. *Barham* main W/T put out of action.
5.02 P.M. *Barham* hit amidships.
5.09 P.M. *Barham* hit aft.
5.11 P.M. *Barham* hit amidships.
5.12 P.M. *Valiant* straddled fore and aft.[31]

In *Warspite*:
Water was pouring through hole in side into sergeants' mess, flooding main deck and going down shell hole to centre engine-room supply trunk. We plugged the supply trunk by big sheets of rubber shored down with deal flats. The body of this shell was found above the engineers' workshop, unexploded. The filling was sticking out like a chock of wood, and a couple of stokers were trying to chip the fuse out. I luckily stopped this little effort.[16]

5.14 P.M. *Malaya* hit starboard side forward about waterline.
5.20 P.M. *Malaya* hit in steam pipe to siren, escape of steam rendering communication with the top impossible for a few minutes.
5.25 P.M. *Malaya* hit in roof of "X" turret—[31]

A midshipman in *Malaya*:

—a very loud crash, followed by a sound like hail . . . we disentangled ourselves, and I looked through the starboard sighting hole at "X" turret, the roof of which had become rather like a badly-made saucer, see-sawing on top of the turret. I caught a vision of the crew inside still going strong, but my interesting report of this was cut short by a salvo from that turret, which precipitated me backwards into the arms of an able seaman.[16]

In *Warspite*:

Went forward to get up fore end, when I was told I was wanted at once as there was a bad fire on the superstructure. A fragment of shell had come through the roof of battery deck and hit the after 6-inch cordite case, containing four charges. As bad luck would have it the cartridge number had a charge half out of the case in his arms. This box and four others exploded. Whole of No. 6 gun's crew were frightfully burnt. The fire was quickly put out.[16]

5.29 P.M.   *Valiant* straddled.
5.30 P.M.   *Malaya* hit starboard side of upper deck.
5.35 P.M.   *Malaya* hit starboard side—[31]

In *Malaya*:

—everything was dark chaos . . . the smell of burnt human flesh, making everybody have a sickly nauseous feeling . . . everything burnt black and bare . . . galley, canteen and drying-room bulkheads blown and twisted into grotesque shapes . . . the whole deck covered by about six inches of water . . . the awful stench of cordite fumes—[16]

In *Warspite*:

—12-inch shell had come through after funnel, through beef-screen,* hit armoured grating over "B" boiler-room. On its way through the beef-screen it had carried a whole sheep with it, which was wedged into the gratings. At first I thought it was a casualty.[16]

* The stowage place for fresh meat.

But the squadron's heavy armour had been built for punishment. Through it all the 15-inch batteries reared up, delivering their steady salvoes.

On the German side the battleships *Grosser Kurfürst* and *Markgraf* were the first to suffer, when *Warspite* and *Malaya* struck them—[22]

A Turret Officer of *Warspite*:

—I distinctly saw two of our salvoes hit the leading German battleship. Sheets of yellow flame went right over her mastheads, and she looked red fore and aft like a burning haystack. Told everybody in the turret that we were doing alright and to keep her going; machinery working like a clockwork mouse.[16]

Then the salvoes reached the battle-cruisers at the head of Hipper's column. Hit by hit, the damage grew.

Seydlitz, *Lützow* and *Derfflinger* were heavily assailed, and *Seydlitz*, already hurt, was seriously injured. A 15-inch shell struck and penetrated through the face armour of her starboard waist turret, putting the right gun out of action and causing heavy casualties. The next projectile entered the after waist turret, which had already been put out of action, and caused a fresh inferno of powder-fire. Still another beat into the port broadside battery, devastating two casemates; a sixth struck full into the right gun of the after turret and destroyed it, while a seventh smashed down upon the roof of the adjacent gunhouse. Half the fighting value of the ship had been remorselessly beaten away.

At 5.30 British shells crashed down upon *Lützow* and *Derfflinger*, the latter being struck twice, the former once—and with this hit Hipper's flagship lost both main and secondary wireless and was without radio communication.[22]

In *Von der Tann*—

von Hase:

—the ship shivered and groaned from the explosions of the shells falling all round her. The first hit was registered between two plates on the starboard side aft. Large fragments of these plates were flung about and driven through the battery deck in several places. The terrific blow at one end caused the ship to oscillate backwards and forwards very violently. The bows and stern dipped in and out five or six times.[25]

5.25 P.M.

Beatty to Battle-Cruisers:

Prepare to renew action.[4]

By 5.40 Admiral Beatty could again make out his adversary in the mist only 14,000 yards away, and the action broke out again in renewed fury. Under the concentrated fire, with the light now in our favour, Admiral Hipper's squadrons began to suffer severely.[11]

In defence the German admiral turned his ships to starboard to steer north-north-east.

The lowering sun appeared through the mist behind Beatty's ships, dazzling the eyes of the German gunners. Beatty's gunners, on the other hand, had the German ships clearly visible. The rumbling broadsides had no sooner begun than a hit was scored upon *Lützow*.

And again Hipper gave ground to the east. It was as though an inflexible pressure were being applied to the head of the German line, forcing it eastward into a massive curve.[22]

This was the time when the Paymaster, who had come on deck for some fresh air, lost his trousers. He was standing on the fore superstructure when "P" turret opened fire and deprived him by its blast of his very necessary garment.[16]

Seizing his advantage and determined that his adversary should not catch even a glimpse of the Grand Fleet, now about to come on the scene, Beatty relentlessly held his easterly course across the German van, bending back the head of their line, and forcing them to retire under the cover of the guns of their own battle fleet.[8]

von Hase:

At the time we did not grasp the object of the enemy's manœuvre. Actually Admiral Beatty, by completely outflanking us in spite of our highest speed, accomplished an excellent tactical manœuvre. He accomplished the famous "crossing the T," compelled us to alter course, and finally brought us into such a position that we were completely enveloped.[25]

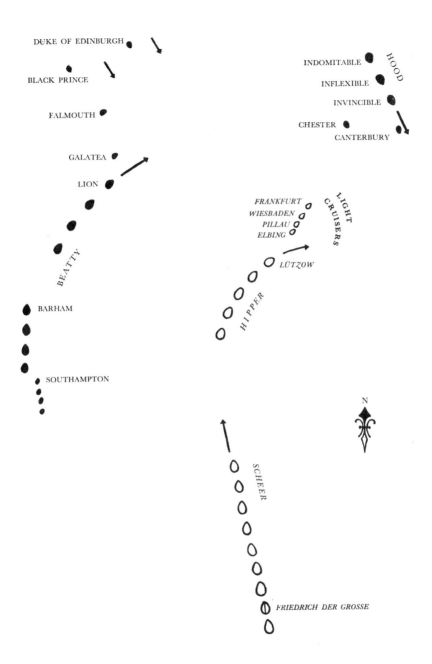

DUKE OF EDINBURGH

BLACK PRINCE

FALMOUTH

INDOMITABLE

INFLEXIBLE

HOOD

INVINCIBLE

CHESTER

CANTERBURY

GALATEA

LION

FRANKFURT
WIESBADEN
PILLAU
ELBING

LIGHT CRUISERS

LÜTZOW

BEATTY

HIPPER

BARHAM

SOUTHAMPTON

N

SCHEER

FRIEDRICH DER GROSSE

73

And this was the moment of Beatty's triumph, for to the north, at a quarter before six, he caught sight of something to make the blood beat— the first outlying cruisers in the vanguard of Jellicoe's Grand Fleet were appearing as tiny specks coming down at 20 knots.[22]

"Hoist Equal Speed Charlie London."

A sharp action involving the advanced forces of the two main fleets marks the first impact between them. The British light cruiser Chester *is roughly handled, and the German* Wiesbaden *disabled.*

Though he has not yet sighted the High Seas Fleet, Jellicoe is now faced with the critical decision of his career: in which direction to deploy his 24 battleships into line. Time is short, and the decision is bafflingly difficult. Mist is spreading; and Beatty's battle-cruisers are crossing Jellicoe's front, the smoke from their funnels and guns adding to the obscurity. Repeated signals of enquiry as to the whereabouts of the German battle-line bring only confusing replies. As the crucial minutes pass, Jellicoe determines to hold on until he is certain of the best direction for deployment.

Beatty is finally able to signal the bearing of the German fleet; and Jellicoe, seeking to "cross the T" of the Germans and to get the best light for gunnery, instantly orders deployment South East by East on the port wing column.

As the British battleships begin to deploy, Rear-Admiral Arbuthnot's cruiser squadron attacks the Wiesbaden, *lying shattered between the fleets but still capable of firing torpedoes. His flagship* Defence *finds herself confronted by Hipper's battle-cruisers and is blown out of the water. Almost simultaneously the* Warspite's *steering-gear jams as she turns to take her place in the British battle-line. Out of control, she swings in a wide circle towards the High Seas Fleet and narrowly escapes destruction.*

From the bridge of Iron Duke *the leading German battleships are sighted through the mist.*

Admiral Hood, in response to the order to support Admiral Beatty, had reached about twenty-five miles ahead of the battle fleet with the 3rd Battle-Cruiser Squadron (*Invincible*, *Inflexible* and *Indomitable*). One of his attached light cruisers, the *Canterbury*, was about five miles further forward; the other, the *Chester*, was the same distance to the westward on his starboard beam, while his four destroyers, *Shark*, *Acasta*, *Ophelia* and *Christopher*, formed his anti-submarine screen ahead.[11]

An officer of *Chester*:
We sighted flashes of guns on our starboard bow, and at once altered to investigate. We increased to full speed, and in a very short time sighted light cruisers.[16]

It was Admiral Boedicker's light cruiser squadron she had run into, as on Hipper's disengaged side it was continuing to the northward, and the ships were the *Frankfurt, Wiesbaden, Pillau* and *Elbing*.[11]

In *Chester*:
The enemy's first salvo fell a good 2,000 yards beyond us, the second from 500 to 700 yards short, and then most of the third came on board. From this point things became pretty brisk, the whole of the enemy light cruiser squadron concentrating on us.[16]

In *Chester*:
We had about five fires, chiefly cordite. One high explosive shell had burst inside the foremost funnel. Two shells burst in the after control position. The range-finder—an instrument weighing several hundredweight—was blown bodily over the side, together with every man of the crew except the Control Officer.[16]

Directly Admiral Hood heard the firing he swung round north-west. In a few minutes our battle-cruisers could see emerging from the mist the *Chester* zigzagging in the storm of shell splashes that were drenching her. A minute later her eager pursuers came suddenly into view. As they passed, his guns crashed into them—[11]

—*Invincible* opened fire on a three-funnelled light cruiser, and was followed by *Inflexible* and *Indomitable*, the squadron being in line ahead in that order—[16]

An officer of *Castor*:

—*Chester* came close across our bows, with four big holes in her along her main deck, and the ship's company cheering through the holes—[12]

—many of the men in her guns' crews had their legs shorn off at the ankles when the decks were swept by a hail of steel fragments from bursting shell. Down the length of her central ammunition passage these wounded men—cheerful Cockneys, for she had a Chatham crew—sat, smoking cigarettes, the bloody stumps of their tourniqueted legs out in front. An hour or so later most of them were dead from shock. Among them was Boy Cornwell, who was awarded a posthumous v.c.[13]

The Germans, in their turn, now tried to escape but they were to suffer heavily before they were swallowed up in the murk. The *Wiesbaden* was hammered to a smoking wreck and, falling out of the line, came to a stop with both engines disabled.[28]

To cover the light cruiser's flight, the German Second Destroyer Flotilla thrust forward to attack Hood. As they drew near they were met by Hood's four destroyers and the light cruiser *Canterbury*. The quick-firing guns spat out as rapidly as they could shoot, torpedoes plunged from tubes, splashed into the water, their tracks instantly lost to sight. The outnumbered British destroyers managed to prevent the attack from reaching Hood's battle-cruisers. The price they paid was the loss of the destroyer *Shark*, whose crippled hulk became the target for ship after ship as the enemy swept down—[22]

William Griffin, Torpedo Coxswain of *Shark*:

—I got wounded in the head and over the right eye, this was when the Forecastle gun's crew were completely blown away, gun and all. The gun-layer, J. Howell, A.B., was wounded in the left leg, and it was about a minute afterwards the captain had his leg shot away, the shell not exploding. C. Hope, A.B., left the gun and assisted the captain—[4]

Able Seaman C. Hope, of *Shark*:

—Captain Jones, seeing the ensign was hanging down the mast, asked what was wrong with the flag, and appeared greatly upset. I climbed and

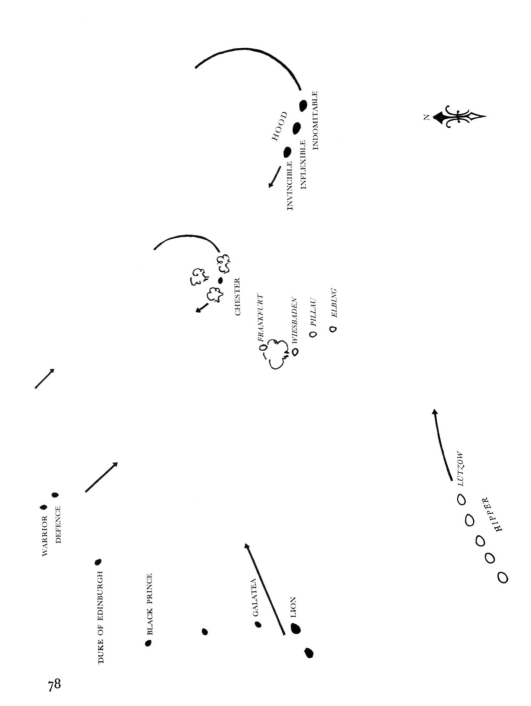

WARRIOR

DEFENCE

DUKE OF EDINBURGH

BLACK PRINCE

GALATEA

LION

HOOD

INVINCIBLE

INFLEXIBLE

INDOMITABLE

N

CHESTER

FRANKFURT

WIESBADEN

PILLAU

ELBING

LÜTZOW

HIPPER

78

unbent the ensign from the staff. I passed it down to Midshipman Smith, who then hoisted it on the yardarm. Commander Jones seemed then to be less worried—[4]

William Griffin:
    —about this time the *Acasta* arrived, and the captain of the *Acasta* asked if he could assist us, and the captain replied don't get sunk over us, we were then with our steering gear and engines out of action—[4]

    —but the *Acasta* had not done yet. Lieutenant-Commander Barron, seeing the *Lützow* coming up on his port quarter, an admirably placed target, turned to attack. With a storm of shell the enemy strove to baffle her attack. Undeterred, Lieut.-Commander Barron fired. The shot seemed to go fairly home with a great explosion, and he sped away with his boat so torn with shell that she could neither stop not steer.[11]

    Shark went down with her flag still flying.
    Upon her, as she lay helpless yet unbeaten, the vast forces of which she formed so small a part were converging to the crisis of the long-foreseen day. Fourteen miles north-west Admiral Jellicoe was coming at high speed towards her, still in cruising order, for as yet no word had come in to tell him where the German battle fleet was, and he was trying vainly to ascertain its position that he might judge how best to deploy.[11]

Report of 1st Battle Squadron:
    The visibility was extremely baffling, partly due to misty clouds appearing and dissolving, and partly due to the layers of smoke from funnels and ships firing—
Report of 4th Battle Squadron:
    —visibility about 5 to 6 miles . . . the light becoming bad—
Report of *St. Vincent*:
    —weather very misty, visibility extreme about 5½ miles—
Report of *Indomitable*:
    —on some bearings one could see 16,000 yards, on others only 2,000.[31]

The Battle Fleet was ready to deploy; its guns were manned, and every man was at his station. The mists had come down, and the columns were becoming grey and ghostly.[29]

Jellicoe's problem was to alter the disposition of his battleships from the order of cruising in six divisions abeam of four ships each (thus presenting the smallest possible target to submarines) into a line of battle (allowing the broadsides of all his 24 battleships to bear on the enemy at the same time).

He was going to deploy into single line ahead; but in which direction?

He had to decide what the relative positions and courses of the two fleets would be when they sighted each other. If Jellicoe crossed Scheer's "T," the broadsides of 24 battleships would bear on the German ships able to reply only with guns firing forward. If Jellicoe misjudged the point and direction of the fleets' contact, Scheer instead would have the decisive advantage of crossing Jellicoe's "T."[3]

5.50 P.M.
  Calliope to Jellicoe:
        Have observed what appears to be flashes of guns S.S.W.
5.50 P.M.
  Southampton to Jellicoe:
        URGENT. PRIORITY.
        Enemy battlefleet has altered course to N.
        Enemy battle-cruisers bear S.W. from enemy battlefleet.
5.50 P.M.
  S.O. 1st Battle Squadron to Jellicoe:
        Gun flashes and heavy gun firing on starboard bow.[4]

Jellicoe (to his staff): "I wish someone would tell me who is firing and what they're firing at."[2]

Jellicoe's account:
Flashes of gunfire were visible from ahead round to the starboard beam, and the noise was heavy and continuous. The conflicting reports added greatly to the perplexity of the situation, and I determined to hold on until matters became clearer.[26]

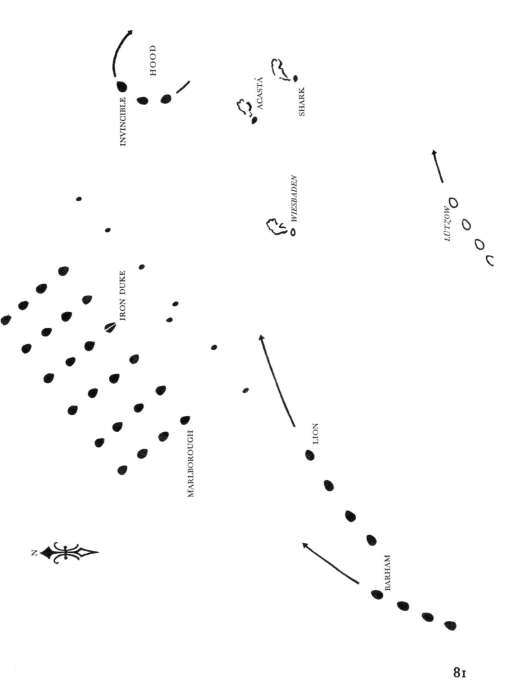

N

INVINCIBLE

HOOD

ACASTA

SHARK

WIESBADEN

LÜTZOW

IRON DUKE

MARLBOROUGH

LION

BARHAM

5.55 P.m.

Jellicoe to *Marlborough*:
> What can you see?

Reply:
> Our battle-cruisers bearing S.S.W. steering east, *Lion* leading ship.[4]

A Midshipman in the foretop of the battleship *Neptune*:

Beatty's battle-cruisers came into sight steaming at high speed to the north-east, and firing heavily towards the southward at an enemy which was out of our sight. The leading ship of Beatty's squadron, *Lion* it was I suppose, seemed to be on fire forward, and the other ships all appeared to have received some damage. The noise rapidly became almost deafening. The *Lion* was leading her squadron across the front of the battle squadrons.[16]

Jellicoe, his small figure now clad in a belted burberry with a scarf knotted at the neck, peered at the hazy line of sea and sky to the south-south-west; in a few moments he and his staff saw *Lion* for themselves at a distance of five miles. She was not a cheering sight; smoke was clearly visible pouring from the port side of her foc'sle, and she and her fellow ships were steaming through German shell splashes that resembled a forest of momentary grey poplars.

Jellicoe instantly signalled Beatty—[3]

6.1 P.M.

Jellicoe to Beatty:
> Where is enemy's battlefleet?[4]

As Beatty raced across the front of the battle fleet, dense smoke pouring from the twelve funnels of his four surviving ships, no flags or searchlight showed on *Lion* to answer Jellicoe's question "Where is the enemy battle fleet?"[3]

Something was evidently wrong, for Admiral Beatty had appeared much further to the westward than his position signals had indicated. Both flag-ships, in fact, were out of their reckoning. The *Lion's* error was nearly seven miles west, and that of the *Iron Duke* over four miles east, so that the cumulative error was about eleven miles. To Admiral Jellicoe it now seemed probable that instead of the enemy being found ahead they would appear a little on his starboard bow. . . . A further effect of the errors in reckoning was that he was likely to get contact twenty minutes sooner than he expected.[11]

6.6 P.M.
    Beatty to Jellicoe:
        Enemy's battle-cruisers bearing S.E.[4]

This did no more than deepen the obscurity. About ten minutes earlier Admiral Jellicoe had learned from Commodore Goodenough (in *Southampton*) that the enemy's battle fleet had altered course to north and that their battle-cruisers bore S.W. from it. On this information it was incomprehensible that the battle-cruisers should have been sighted first, and at his wits' end to fathom the situation the Commander-in-Chief repeated to Admiral Beatty:[11]

6.10 P.M.
    Jellicoe to Beatty:
        Where is enemy's battlefleet?[4]

At the moment the *Lion* had no enemy in sight. There was no immediate answer, and precious minutes went by with no further light to determine the right direction for deployment.[11]

Commodore von Schoultz, observer from the Imperial Russian Navy, in the battleship *Hercules*:
Between us and the squadron on our port beam is a Norwegian sailing ship which rolls in our wash as we pass. The sails flap lightly to the movement of the ship. A chance eye witness of an event in world history. What would the American film companies not give to have a photographer on board this ship?[33]

On *Iron Duke's* forebridge, among his staff, Jellicoe kept his counsel. As the margin of time narrowed and vanished, like the distance between the invisible fleets; as two great national rivalries, expressed by sixteen years of preparation, converged to collision point, Jellicoe himself reached the end of the line along which he had been steadily moving since that day in 1876 when he first put on the blue coat of the Royal Navy. He stood staring impassively ahead, showing no sign of the extreme test of nerve he was undergoing. For he was determined not to make a premature and possibly wrong deployment on the basis of vague information; he was going to hold on at 18 knots until he knew exactly the bearing of the enemy.[3]

There was not an instant to lose . . . the two hostile fleets were rushing upon each other; battle-cruisers, cruisers and destroyers were hurrying to their battle stations, and the vessels steaming across his front were shutting out all beyond in an impenetrable pall of funnel smoke. Above all was the roar of battle both ahead and to starboard, and in this blind distraction Admiral Jellicoe had to make the decision on which the fortunes of his country hung.[11]

von Schoultz in *Hercules*:
I was standing on the bridge beside Clinton Baker,* impatiently awaiting a signal to deploy. Neither of us spoke, for fear of betraying the anxiety we both felt as to the approaching decision.[33]

Jellicoe's account:
As the evidence accumulated that the enemy's Battle Fleet was on our starboard side, but on a bearing well before the beam of the *Iron Duke*, the point for decision was whether to form line of battle on the starboard or on the port wing column. My first and natural impulse was to form on the starboard wing column in order to bring the Fleet into action at the earliest possible moment, but it became increasingly apparent that the High Seas Fleet was in such close proximity and on such a bearing as to create obvious disadvantages in such a movement.

The German destroyers would be ahead of their Battle Fleet, and it was clear that, owing to the mist, the operations of destroyers attacking from a commanding position in the van would be much facilitated.

If the German ships were as close as seemed probable, there was considerable danger of the 1st Battle Squadron, and especially the *Marlborough's* Division, being severely handled by the concentrated fire of the High Seas Fleet before the remaining divisions could get into line to assist.

* Captain of *Hercules*.

It appeared, from the supposed position of the High Seas Fleet, that the van of the enemy would have a very considerable "overlap" if line were formed on the starboard wing division, whereas this would not be the case with deployment on the port wing column.[28]

But at 6.14, four minutes after he had repeated his urgent enquiry as to where the enemy's battle fleet was, all doubt was set at rest—[11]

6.14 P.M.
Beatty to Jellicoe:
    Have sighted enemy's battlefleet bearing S.S.W.[4]

Dreyer in *Iron Duke*:
    I was standing amidships at the standard compass on the manœuvring platform, when at 6.14 p.m. I heard the signalman calling each word of Beatty's reply to Jellicoe's repeated demand, as flashed by a searchlight in the *Lion*: "HAVE SIGHTED ENEMY'S BATTLE FLEET. BEARING S.S.W."
    I then heard at once the sharp, distinctive step of the Commander-in-Chief approaching—he had steel strips on his heels. He stepped quickly on to the platform round the compasses and looked in silence at the magnetic compass card for about twenty seconds. I watched his keen, brown, weather-beaten face with tremendous interest, wondering what he would do. With iron nerve he had pressed on through the mist with his twenty-four huge ships until the last possible moment, so as to get into effective range and make the best tactical manœuvre after obtaining news of the position of the enemy battle fleet. I realised as I watched him that he was as cool and unmoved as ever.[13]

Jellicoe's notes:
    I was guided in my deployment by two factors. *One* was to cross the T. *Two* to get the best light for gunnery. During the moments when I was making the decision as to which wing to deploy on, I directed Dreyer to let me know in which direction the light was most favourable. To meet both conditions I deployed on the port wing column.[14]

85

Dreyer:

He looked up and broke the silence with the order in his crisp, clear-cut voice to Commander Woods, the Fleet Signal Officer, who was standing a little abaft of me:

"Hoist equal-speed pendant S.E."

Woods said: "Would you make it a point to port, sir, so that they will know it is on the port-wing column?"

Jellicoe replied at once: "Very well. Hoist equal-speed pendant S.E. by E."

Woods then called over the bridge rail to the signal boatswain: "Hoist equal-speed Charlie London."*

We had not yet sighted any German vessel from the *Iron Duke*.[13]

6.15 P.M.

Jellicoe to British Battle Fleet:

> EQUAL SPEED C.L.[4]
>
> Meaning:
>
> The column nearest S.E. by E. is to alter course in succession to that point of the compass, the remaining columns altering course leading ships together the rest in succession so as to form astern of that column, maintaining the speed of the fleet.

von Schoultz in *Hercules*:

"All right," says Clinton Baker at my side, and goes to the conning-tower. The others also go to their action stations. I am left alone on the bridge with two seamen in charge of a navigational range-finder.[33]

Dreyer:

While some ships were still answering the signal, Jellicoe said to me: "Dreyer, commence the deployment."

I at once blew two short blasts on the siren (the deployment being to port) and ordered the helm to be put over. The commanders of adjacent columns, who were watching for this, immediately did likewise; each blew two short blasts and put the helm over.[13]

* "C.L." denoting S.E. by E.

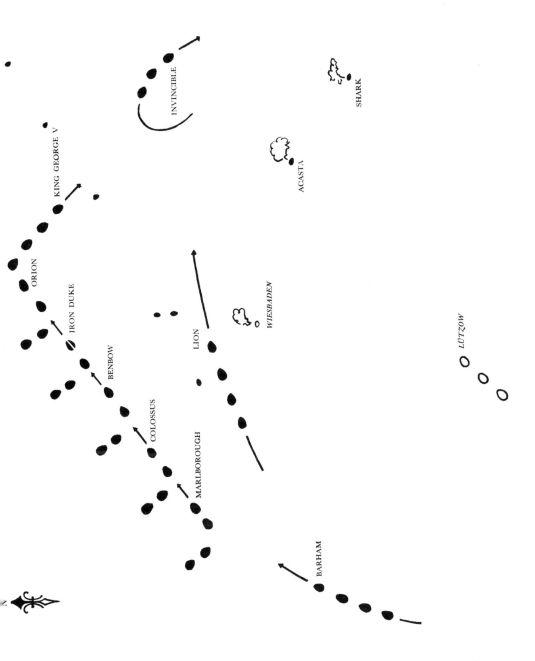

N

INVINCIBLE

SHARK

KING GEORGE V

ACASTA

ORION

IRON DUKE

WIESBADEN

BENBOW

LION

LÜTZOW

COLOSSUS

MARLBOROUGH

BARHAM

87

The manœuvre was as follows: the port wing division continued to steam in the general direction south-south-east, while in succession the other divisions turned first into line north-north-east, and then again south-south-east following the port wing division.[3]

In *Iron Duke*:

We had still not yet sighted a German ship, but they were obviously very close. From 6.20, some five minutes after deploying, all the battleships were in single line, with a kink of 67° in it to starboard, where one ship at a time was at the turning point. All ships, with their turret guns, could cover a large area in which the enemy might be sighted.[13]

In *Neptune*:

I noticed that several ships were flying three or four ensigns from various parts of the rigging, and, sure enough, the squeak of our halliard blocks announced that we were following suit. I don't know who started it, but in about ten minutes the air seemed to be thick with white ensigns, large and small, silk and bunting, hoisted wherever halliards could be rove.[16]

Proud and stately, each grey dreadnought came into her place in the line in turn, and wheeled, her battle-flags whipping from her trucks, snowy white flags with the livid cross of St. George and the bright British union. At the head of the line *King George V*, *Ajax*, *Centurion*, *Erin*, *Orion*, *Monarch*, *Conqueror*, and *Thunderer*. In the centre, *Iron Duke*, *Royal Oak*, *Superb*, *Canada*, *Benbow*, *Bellerophon*, *Temeraire* and *Vanguard*. At the rear, *Colossus*, *Collingwood*, *Neptune*, *St. Vincent*, *Marlborough*, *Revenge*, *Hercules* and *Agincourt*.[22]

But now the bait of the *Wiesbaden* was to lure a British unit to destruction.

The heavy cruisers of Rear-Admiral Arbuthnot's Squadron had opened fire on her at 6.5 p.m. and, pressing on at full speed to cross the bows of the *Lion*, Arbuthnot's flagship *Defence* with the *Warrior* and *Black Prince* moved into the area between the two fleets to give the coup-de-grace to the wounded *Wiesbaden*—[28]

In the cruiser *Warrior*:

—as she was still in a position favourable for firing torpedoes at our battle-cruisers, we, *Defence* and *Warrior*, continued hitting her again and

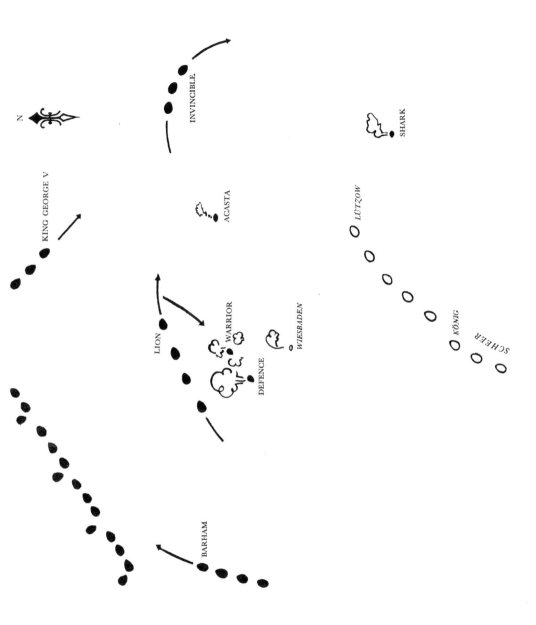

N

KING GEORGE V

INVINCIBLE

ACASTA

SHARK

LÜTZOW

WARRIOR

WIESBADEN

LION

DEFENCE

KÖNIG

SCHEER

BARHAM

again with our port guns. I remember remarking to the Navigator, "We have never had a practice concentration of fire go off so smoothly."[16]

As they pounded the almost defenceless ship, out of the mist and smoke to the southward loomed Hipper's battle-cruisers and the Third Squadron of German battleships at the head of their line. Baulked from seeing any other target, every German ship opened a smothering fire on the British cruisers.[28]

From the destroyer *Obedient*:
Three quick salvoes reached *Defence*, the first one over, the next one short, and the third all hit. The ship heeled to the blow, but quickly righted herself and steamed on again. Then almost immediately followed three more salvoes. Again the first was over, the second short, and the third a hit. At once the ship was lost to sight in an enormous black cloud—[16]

From the battleship *Colossus*:
—a tremendous belch of vivid flame and dense black smoke, from which some dark object, possibly a boat or a funnel, was hurled through space, twirling like a gigantic Catherine-wheel—[16]

From *Neptune*:
—the fore-top fell with a sickening splash into the water and then the *Warrior*, herself damaged, listing to starboard and in places on fire, raced over the spot where the *Defence* had been only a moment before, through the smoke cloud of *Defence's* explosion—[16]

From *Warspite*:
—thirty seconds elapsed, the smoke lifted, and for 5 seconds we saw her bottom, and then she slid down to the bottom of the sea. As far as I could see not a vestige of wreckage remained on the surface.[16]

Just twenty-four hours earlier, Arbuthnot had been playing tennis with Lady Jellicoe, ashore at Cromarty.[22]

King Hall in *Southampton*:

As the enemy redoubled their efforts to destroy the *Warrior*, a most extraordinary incident amazed both sides.

The *Warspite*, just ahead of us, altered course to starboard and proceeded straight for the centre of the enemy line. As she continued to plunge forward towards the Germans the tornado of fire lifted from the *Warrior*, hovered as it seemed in space, and fell with a crash about the *Warspite*.

The *Warrior*, burning in several places, battered and wrecked, with steam escaping from many broken pipes, dragged slowly out of the battle to the westward.

I watched the *Warspite* and wondered what her amazing behaviour portended—[24]

In *Warspite*:

—we were turning to form astern of the Grand Fleet battle line, and the helm was apparently put over too quickly and jammed. We swung to starboard under *Valiant's* stern, and continued swinging round towards the enemy, getting very close to them. We continued swinging round until we were on a westerly course, when the Captain managed to steady the ship by working the screws. We got very heavily hit, and everybody thought we had gone. . . .

. . . so terrific was the noise of the bursting shell that no one in the conning tower could hear the Captain's orders, added to which the Navigating Officer was temporarily blinded by our gun flash, with the result that the Captain himself had to work the telegraphs and use the voice tubes—[16]

King Hall:

—I should guess that she had reached a position about 8,000 yards from the German line when to our relief she slowly turned round, and still lashing out viciously with all her 15-inch guns she rejoined the British lines.*[24]

Between the fleets lay the blazing *Wiesbaden*, wreathed in smoke; at the rear of the line, the cloud of the explosion in which the *Defence* had perished hung like a pall over the water. The deployment on the port wing had

---

* But owing to her damage and to further steering difficulties she was ordered to withdraw from the battle and return to Rosyth.

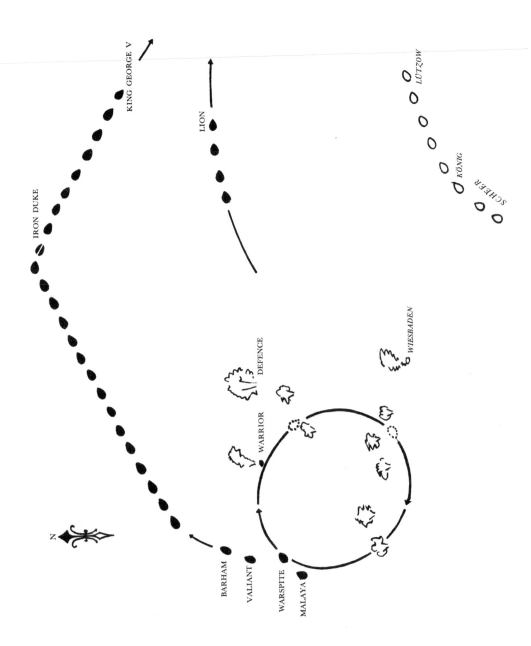

committed the battle-cruisers to crossing the front to take up their station ahead, and as they passed they, too, had to mask the fire of some of the ships in the van—[29]

—Beatty's battle-cruisers, steaming at high speeds, were pouring dense smoke-clouds into the area between the opposing fleets. Words can hardly describe the confusion caused by the junction of the two British fleets at "Windy Corner." That not a single collision occurred in that melee was due to the marvellous seamanship of the captains—[18]

—the whole surface of the sea was heaving up and down in a confused swell, which was caused by the wash created by the two hundred odd ships which were moving about at high speeds—[24]

—there was much bunching up of ships in the rear of the line. *Marlborough* and other ships had to reduce to 8 knots and *St. Vincent* had to stop for a short time. Owing to the haze and the enemy's smoke, organised distribution of fire was out of the question; individual ships selected their own targets.[4]

Dreyer in the *Iron Duke*:
Three ships whose silhouettes corresponded to those of the most recent German type of *König* class battleships came in sight, 20° before the starboard beam, range 12,000 yards.

Jellicoe said to me, "Dreyer, I think it is time for you to go to your station in the conning-tower."[13]

"Gefechtskehrtwendung nach Steuerbord."

During the British deployment a duel takes place between Rear-Admiral Hood's 3rd Battle-Cruiser Squadron, at the head of the line, and the German battle-cruisers. Invincible, *flagship of the squadron, is sunk.*

Jellicoe's deployment crosses the German T, but the effectiveness of the British gunnery is reduced by mist and smoke. But as the British line circles on to a southerly course, Scheer realises that he is faced with the entire battleship strength of the Grand Fleet. He evades envelopment by a turn-away movement involving a simultaneous swing-round of all his ships. The High Seas Fleet disappears westward behind mist and smoke-screens, and the British lose contact with it.

Scheer then turns eastward again, hoping to pass astern of the British fleet in the general direction of his home bases. He swings his ships about—but finds himself steering straight for the centre of the British battle-line. His T is crossed again; and the Grand Fleet opens a furious cannonade upon his battleships.

The High Seas Fleet is now in peril of rout or destruction. Scheer immediately executes another turn-away, at the same time ordering his battle-cruisers to cover his retreat by charging the enemy without regard for consequences. The German battle-cruisers embark on a death-ride towards the British line.

Scheer also launches his destroyers in a torpedo attack; and Jellicoe, convinced that his first duty is to conserve his battleships, turns them away so as to present only their beams, rather than their full lengths, to the German torpedoes. The manœuvre is successful in that all torpedoes are avoided. But by the time the British have regained their southward course the German fleet has again vanished behind mist and smoke. Though intermittent contact with parts of it are re-established, no further general action ensues before nightfall.

Scheer decides that during the night he will strike eastward for home at all costs.

As the cloud of smoke and flame in which the *Defence* had perished died away, the leading ships of the German line could see, out of the grey beyond, an interminable line of huge ships stretching across their course with both ends of it lost in the mist. For Admiral Scheer, who believed that our fleet was operating in dispersed detachments, the sight came with a shock of surprise.[11]

Marlborough:
 Picked up as target an enemy battleship of the *Kaiser* class—
 —Opened fire at 6.17—
 —When the splash for the fifth salvo was reported I saw four explosions with a red flame—[16]

Dreyer in *Iron Duke:*
 —by voice-pipe I asked Jellicoe for permission to fire at the leading *König*—
 —He told me to wait until he was satisfied that it was an enemy ship—
 —At 6.30 he told me to open fire at her.[13]

Scheer's account:
 It was now quite obvious that we were confronted by a large portion of the English fleet. The entire arc stretching from north to east was a sea of fire. The flash from the muzzles of the guns was distinctly seen through the mist and smoke on the horizon, though the ships themselves were not distinguishable.[32]

First two, then four, then six and eight, nine British battleships began to respond to the fire, joining the cannonade as they wheeled into the battle-line. The High Seas Fleet, appearing and disappearing into the gloom seven miles away, was the target—ships seen by the gunners for the first time.[22]

von Schoultz in *Hercules:*
 Just at this moment we fired our first salvo . . . the heavy shock lifted me involuntarily into the air . . .
 . . . my attention is distracted by enemy shells shrieking over the ship.

I see a splash very close to our port side which gives me a thorough shower bath. Other shells are falling to starboard of us. The salvo is straddling us. The German gunnery must be particularly good—[33]

—*Hercules* on sighting three enemy battleships of the *Kaiser* class indistinctly through the mist, fired seven or eight salvoes at the ship that appeared most visible—
    —*Revenge* fired salvoes at an enemy battleship—
    —*Agincourt* opened fire on an enemy battleship—hits obtained on this ship—[31]

In *Agincourt*:
    —the deployment placed *Agincourt* tail ship of the battle line, but we had all the fun our end—

Warspite:
    —I saw *Agincourt* firing like blazes—

A cruiser:
    —as we were dashing across the bows of *Agincourt* she fired a salvo over us which fairly lifted us in the water . . . I felt as if my head was blown off—

Malaya:
    —*Agincourt*, looking more like a Brock's Benefit than a battleship, as she poured out salvoes from her broadside of fourteen 12-inch guns—[16]

Benbow:
    —opened fire at a battle-cruiser—

Colossus:
    —opened fire—three salvoes—

Orion:
    —fired at a *Kaiser* class—after four salvoes observed flames near the enemy's after turret—

Monarch:
—fired at the leading *König*—straddle—

Thunderer:
—fired at a *Kaiser* class—straddling her with second and third salvoes—the enemy was then seen blazing for the whole length of her quarter deck.[31]

von Schoultz in *Hercules*:
I decide to go to the upper bridge again, and there find our bugler, a youth of fifteen. When I ask him what he is doing there I notice tears in his eyes and realise that the poor lad, whose duty it is to pass on signals, is terrified by the gunfire and probably still more by the loneliness, for not a soul is to be seen on deck.[33]

The German van was faced by the belching guns of an interminable line of heavy ships extending from north-west to north-east, whilst salvo followed salvo, almost without intermission, an impression which gained in power from the almost complete inability of the German ships to reply to this fire, as not one of the British dreadnoughts could be made out through the smoke and fumes.[21]

Dreyer:
In the *Iron Duke's* conning-tower I was watching our very accurate firing at the *König*. Our Gunnery Officer, who was standing a few feet abaft me, said he heard me saying, "Beautiful, beautiful," like a rose-grower at a show.[18]

The Third Battle-Cruiser Squadron, led by Admiral Hood in the *Invincible*, took up station about two miles ahead of Beatty. The German battle-cruisers suddenly appeared out of the mist. Hood immediately opened fire—[8]

—on *Invincible's* bridge, the Admiral was delightedly watching the excellent shooting of his Gunnery Officer, Commander Danreuther. Calling up the voice-pipe, he exclaimed, "Your firing is very good. Keep at it as quickly as you can. Every shot is telling."
Hardly had he spoken when—[28]

von Hase in *Derfflinger*:

—"Range 9,000!" roared Leading Seaman Hänel.

"9,000—salvoes—fire!" I ordered.

"Over. Two hits!" called out Lieutenant-Commander von Stosch.

I gave the order "100 down. Rapid!" and thirty seconds after the first salvo the second left the guns.

I observed two short splashes and two hits.

Then for the third time we witnessed the dreadful spectacle that we had already seen in the case of the *Queen Mary* and the *Defence*—[25]

—*Invincible* was hit by a salvo amidships . . . great tongues of flame shot out from her riven side, the masts collapsed, the ship broke in two, and an enormous pall of black smoke rose to the sky—[8]

von Hase:

—from the parting sections of the ship coal dust spurted in all directions, fresh explosions followed, and behind this murky shroud our enemy vanished from sight.

I shouted into the telephone "Our enemy has blown up!" and above the din of the battle a great cheer thundered through the ship and was transmitted to the fore-control by all the gunnery telephones and flashed from one gun position to another—[25]

From *Indomitable*:

—I saw the two ends of a ship standing perpendicularly above water, the ship appearing to have broken in halves amidships, each half resting on the bottom. My gunlayer took her for a Hun, and the crew cheered, but I could read the name *Invincible* on the stern—[16]

From *Lion*:

—observed some survivors on a raft who cheered the *Lion* as she passed. Their spirit remained unshaken by this dreadful experience, although their hope of rescue was slight. Fortunately for them the destroyer *Badger* happened to be near at hand, so Beatty ordered her—[8]

Beatty to *Badger*:

Pick up survivors from wreck on starboard side.[4]

In *Badger*:

We could see the water all round thick with flotsam and jetsam. We spotted a raft on which were four men, and on the bridge they spotted two other survivors in the water. I lowered and sent away the whaler, with our gunner in charge armed with a service revolver. The Captain brought the ship alongside the raft, and I waited to receive German survivors. Judge of my surprise, when the raft was almost alongside, to see a Commander R.N., a Lieutenant R.N., and two seamen ratings on it. I quickly sent the armed guard away and apologised to the Commander,* who only treated it as a good joke. He assured us that he hadn't a scratch on his whole body, and that he had merely—as he put it—stepped into the water when the fore-top came down.[16]

The British battle fleet had almost completed its deployment, and although it was baffled by patches of mist and hanging smoke, nearly all ships were firing and getting hits. The head of the German line was already being smashed in.

Admiral Scheer thus found himself in an awkward predicament.[11]

Scheer was an unusual man. He was as cool as ice, and just as unperturbed. His reactions were essentially direct and simple. Many writers in trying to attribute to him brilliant and far-reaching plans have misjudged Scheer and deceived themselves. "While the battle is progressing a leader cannot obtain a really clear picture, especially at long ranges. He acts and feels according to his impressions."[18]

With only a German fleet speed of 17 knots in contrast to the British fleet speed of 20 knots, Admiral Scheer could not possibly hope to gain safety by flight. It was at this crisis that the carefully rehearsed German fleet manœuvre of evasion prepared for exactly such a situation, to break away from the pressure of a stronger enemy fleet, stood the German Commander-in-Chief in good stead.[20]

Scheer's account:

I decided to turn our line and bring it on to an opposite course—[32]

* It was Danreuther, the Gunnery Officer.

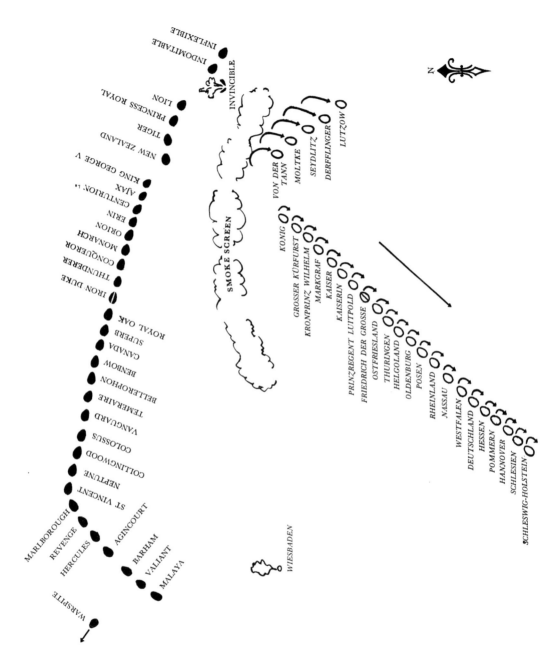

INDOMITABLE
INFLEXIBLE
INVINCIBLE
LION
PRINCESS ROYAL
TIGER
NEW ZEALAND
KING GEORGE V
AJAX
CENTURION *L*
ERIN
ORION
MONARCH
CONQUEROR
THUNDERER
IRON DUKE
ROYAL OAK
SUPERB
CANADA
BENBOW
BELLEROPHON
TEMERAIRE
VANGUARD
COLOSSUS
COLLINGWOOD
NEPTUNE
ST VINCENT
AGINCOURT
MARLBOROUGH
REVENGE
HERCULES
BARHAM
VALIANT
MALAYA
WARSPITE

SMOKE SCREEN

LUTZOW
DERFFLINGER
SEYDLITZ
MOLTKE
VON DER TANN

KONIG
GROSSER KÜRFURST
KRONPRINZ WILHELM
MARKGRAF
KAISER
KAISERIN
PRINZREGENT LUITPOLD
FRIEDRICH DER GROSSE
OSTFRIESLAND
THURINGEN
HELGOLAND
OLDENBURG
POSEN
RHEINLAND
NASSAU
WESTFALEN
DEUTSCHLAND
HESSEN
POMMERN
HANNOVER
SCHLESIEN
SCHLESWIG-HOLSTEIN

WIESBADEN

N

6.35 P.M.

Scheer to High Seas Fleet:

Gefechtskehrtwendung nach Steuerbord.[23]

Battle turn-away to starboard.

This German rehearsed manœuvre was a simultaneous "swing around" of all the ships of a fleet to turn the line and bring it into an opposite course, executed under the cover of dense smoke screens for concealment.[20]

Captain Redlich immediately turned the *Westfalen*, rear ship of Squadron I, to course west. He was followed by the entire squadron. The ships of Squadron III then followed. The *Markgraf*, with one engine out of commission, had difficulty in maintaining her station—[18]

Scheer:

—the swing round was carried out in excellent style. At our peace manœuvres great importance was always attached to their being carried out on a curved line and every means employed to ensure the working of the signals. The trouble spent was now repaid.[32]

The effect was all he could desire. In two or three minutes his fleet, already only visible from the British ships by glimpses, had disappeared, and all firing ceased.[11]

In fact none of the British commanders realised what had taken place under cover of that smoke screen.[19]

The German appearance and disappearance had taken place before the British deployment was fully completed. Only at 6.45 was Jellicoe's massive evolution finished, with all his ships on a south-easterly course. Now thirty-three British capital ships were formed into one unbroken column eleven miles long, the battle-cruisers at the tip, then the twenty-four dreadnoughts of the Grand Fleet proper, and at the rear the three dreadnoughts of the Fifth Battle Squadron. The innumerable light cruisers and destroyers had taken up their battle and scouting positions at van and rear.

At 6.50 the gunfire had completely died away. The guns were lifted expectantly—[22]

von Schoultz, in *Hercules*:

—the bridge is still deserted, and the ship drives forward in uncanny silence. Our giant guns stretch far over the side towards the enemy. A dense veil of smoke drifts towards us from ahead.[33]

In *Indomitable*:

Should it be my good fortune to be engaged in another action, I shall take care that only one gramophone is taken into the turret. In my turret we had two, one in the gunhouse and one in the working chamber, and during every lull in the action these two started playing simultaneously. The result was one of the real horrors of the war.[16]

Jellicoe's notes:

I imagined the disappearance of the enemy to be due merely to the thickening of the mist, but after a few minutes had elapsed it became clear that there must be some other reason and at 6.44 I hauled up one point to south-east and at 6.55 four more points to south, signalling at the same time—[14]

6.55 P.M.
Jellicoe to *Marlborough*:
Can you see any enemy battleships?

Reply: No.[4]

At the moment of *Invincible's* destruction, Admiral Hipper was turning the German battle-cruisers away from the enemy to follow after the retiring High Seas Fleet.

Lützow, his flagship, had received such injuries that she was struggling to stay afloat, and had all but lost her power to steam—she and *Invincible* had done for each other.[22]

It was plain that circumstances had made it essential for the group staff to leave the *Lützow* and another ship must be chosen as flagship. Yet Hipper issued no orders. It was the first time that he had had nothing to say.

His First Staff Officer, Commander Raeder, went up to him and said:

"We can't lead the squadron from the *Lützow* any more, Your Excellency."

"But I can't leave my flagship."

"We're unable to signal by wireless and anyhow our speed isn't enough."

"No doubt. But my flagship."

"The squadron needs Your Excellency."

Hipper seemed to have an electric shock. In a flash he was the Hipper of old.[35]

The destroyer-leader G 39, superbly handled by Lieutenant von Loefen, ran alongside the *Lützow*.

"Get away to *Seydlitz* as fast as you can so that I can take over command again," was Hipper's order.[36]

When the racing G 39 reached the *Seydlitz* there was a hole as big as a barn door in her bows and hundreds of tons of water could be heard gurgling inside her. Worst of all, her wireless was also out of action.

There was nothing for it but to move on to the *Von der Tann*. But even she was hardly fit to play the part of flagship. Her heavy guns were as good as out of action.

Hipper—anxious not to fail his squadron—decided to try his luck with *Moltke*. "I've got a thousand tons of water on board," was the report of her commander, Captain von Karpf, "but otherwise I'm fit for your purpose."

Moltke stopped. G 39 was about to lay alongside—[35]

But now ensued one of those astounding events utterly outside the bounds of reasonable expectation, which have often been the turning points of history. No sooner did Scheer, after steaming for about twenty minutes to the westward, find himself free, than he turned each ship about right-handed and again steamed eastward. What was his purpose?[10]

Scheer, in private comment afterwards:

The fact is I had no definite object. When I noticed that the British pressure had quite ceased and that the fleet remained intact in my hands, I turned back under the impression that the action could not end in this way, and that I ought to seek contact with the enemy again.[30]

A course to the east would give a fair chance of crossing astern of the (British) main body. Further, the course would carry him past the *Wiesbaden*, whose crew he was bent on rescuing, and once clear to the eastward he would have his enemy at gunnery advantage against the western horizon. From such a position, moreover, each time he launched his destroyers to attack he would be driving the enemy further off the line of retreat. Such a device was much more to be expected from his ability than the incredible folly of which it was his humour to accuse himself.[11]

6.55 P.M.
Scheer to High Seas Fleet:
   Gefechtskehrtwendung nach Steuerbord.[23]
   Ships about, to starboard.

The German battle fleet was swung round 16 points together to an easterly course. It was now heading straight into the centre of the arc formed by the British fleet. In a few minutes the leading squadron and battle-cruisers would be threatened with envelopment and the concentrated fire of practically the whole Grand Fleet. The High Seas Fleet seemed to be rushing headlong to destruction.[29]

von Schoultz in *Hercules*:
   At first, the advancing German Battle Fleet could scarcely be distinguished. The van was led by the battle-cruiser *Derfflinger*, followed by *Moltke*, *Seydlitz* and *Von der Tann*; then four ships of the *König* class; then the *Friedrich der Grosse* and the remaining divisions.[33]

The Grand Fleet's broadsides spoke, spreading forward as the enemy became visible—long, thunderous rumble of guns, heavy and portentous, rising and falling in a beat of sound like the booming of titanic surf, a sound that spoke of the histories of nations and the chronicle of man. Above the deep fury of the turrets came the splitting staccato of the secondary guns— [22]

7.12 P.M.
Marlborough:
   —opened fire—14 salvoes in 6 minutes—6th, 12th, 13th and 14th all distinct hits—[4]

Monarch:

    —opened fire at a *König* class—obtained hits—

Iron Duke:

    —fired four salvoes at a *Helgoland* battleship—

Colossus:

    —fired five salvoes—two straddled—four direct hits—[31]

von Schoultz:

—the ship drives forward—trembling and quivering under the shock of her own salvoes—ahead of us steams the *Revenge*, astern the *Agincourt*—[33]

Centurion:

    —at a *Kaiser* class—

Royal Oak:

    —at a battle-cruiser—

King George V:

    —opened fire on the leading enemy ship—

Temeraire:

    —at a battle-cruiser—

Superb:

    —at a battle-cruiser—[31]

In *Neptune:*

—a marvellously impressive spectacle as salvo after salvo rolled out along the line, adding to the fearful din which the enemy's shells were already making—[16]

—the Germans were in the most unfavourable and dangerous situation imaginable. Jellicoe enjoyed the overwhelming advantages of position, visibility, and numbers. . . . No commander-in-chief of history could have been under such compressed tension as was Scheer during those few minutes when the fate of the world hung in the balance—[18]

Agincourt:

    —registering hits on a battleship of the *Kaiser* class—

Marlborough:
> —large cloud of grey and white smoke appeared near the fore-mast—two hits clearly seen under the bridge—

Colossus:
> —at least four direct hits, two on the waterline—enemy burst into flames, listed and disappeared in the flame, mist and smoke.[31]

To make matters worse, while the German ships were showing up clearly against the glow of the westering sun, only intermittently and dimly could they see their enemy.

Once again, Scheer could only save himself by precipitate retreat.[28]

7.13 P.M.
Scheer, urgently, to the German Battle-Cruisers:
> Grosse Kreuzer Gefechtswendung rein in den Feind. Ran.
> Battle-cruisers charge the enemy without regard for consequences. Ram.

7.16 P.M.
Scheer, urgently, to High Seas Fleet:
> Gefechtskehrtwendung nach Steuerbord.[23]
> Battle turn-away to starboard.

On Hipper's orders, G 39 turned away at right angles from the *Moltke*. Masses of destroyers hurtled past. Everything must be staked on a mighty effort to compel Jellicoe to turn, a desperate throw to break the iron ring of British superiority. And in the centre of the drama was Hipper in a destroyer.

Round and about him the water was being hurled up in great fountains. The enemy guns thundered. It was as if the sky were raining bolts of steel. The ships rushed on leaving foaming wakes behind them. Mountainous waves rolled over each other.

Hipper took a deep breath and let his eyes roam over the scene. And now his critical faculties asserted themselves and be began to reflect whether the attack should have taken this particular form. The days of ramming tactics were over—[35]

BARHAM

MARLBOROUGH

COLOSSUS

BENBOW

IRON
DUKE

ORION

KING
GEORGE V

LION

DERFFLINGER

KÖNIG

KAISER

FRIEDRICH DER GROSSE

POSEN

DEUTSCHLAND

HANNOVER

N

WIESBADEN

von Hase in *Derfflinger*:

—the signalman on our bridge read the message aloud: "And ram! The ships will fight to the death."

Without moving an eyelid the Captain gave the order: "Full speed ahead. Course S.E." Followed by the *Seydlitz, Moltke* and *Von der Tann* we headed straight for the enemy's van.

Salvo after salvo fell around us, hit after hit struck our ship. A shell pierced the armour of "Caesar" turret and exploded inside. The turret commander, Lieut.-Commander von Boltenstern, had both his legs torn off and with him nearly the whole gun crew was killed. . . . The burning cartridge-cases emitted great tongues of flame which shot up out of the turret as high as a house. The huge tapering flames killed everyone within their reach.

A shell pierced the roof of "Dora" turret. The same horrors ensued. From both after turrets great flames were now spurting, mingled with clouds of yellow smoke, two ghastly pyres. . . I felt a clutch at my heart when I thought of what the conditions must be in the interior of the ship. . . . A terrific roar, a tremendous explosion and then darkness. . . . The whole conning-tower seemed to be hurled into the air. . . . Poisonous greenish-yellow gases poured through the aperture into our control. I called out: "Down gas-masks!" and immediately every man pulled down his gas-mask over his face. . . . Whole sheets of the deck were hurled through the air, a tremendous concussion threw overboard everything that could be moved . . . we could scarcely see anything of the enemy, who were disposed in a great semi-circle round us. All we could see was the great reddish-gold flames spurting from the guns. . . . The flashes from the muzzles looked like the opening of two wide blazing eyes and suddenly I realised where I had seen something of the sort. Sascha Schneider's picture "The feeling of dependence" had created an impression of something similar to what I was now experiencing. It depicts a black monster of shadowy outline, opening and shutting its smouldering eyes and fixing a chained human form, which awaits the final embrace.[25]

When Admiral Scheer made his "death ride" signal to his battle-cruisers he also launched his destroyers to attack; these rushed forward with determination. The attack promised to be a formidable one—[1]

Beatty to Battlefleet:
Enemy's destroyers are approaching to attack.[4]

—they were making a very heavy smoke screen, and were never on the same course for more than about a minute at a time, turning, twisting, wriggling, and disappearing into their own smoke, only to reappear again almost immediately at a different place.[16]

Judging that they were about to fire their torpedoes, the Commander-in-Chief decided to turn away.[29]

Jellicoe had always believed that in a fleet action the Germans would make every possible use of mines and torpedoes. In a memorandum of 30 October 1914 he had informed the Admiralty that in such an event he would take evasive action:

> I desire particularly to draw the attention of Their Lordships to this point since it may be deemed a refusal of battle . . . I feel that such tactics, if not understood, may bring odium upon me, but it is quite within the bounds of possibility that half our Battle Fleet might be disabled by under-water attack.[5]

The Admiralty had expressed their "full confidence in your contemplated conduct of the Fleet in action."

7.22 P.M.
Jellicoe to Battlefleet and attached cruisers:
> Subdivisions separately alter course in succession two points away from Enemy preserving their formation.

Jellicoe to 4th Light Cruiser Squadron:
> 4th L.C.S. prepare to attack the torpedo vessels of Enemy. Proceed at your utmost speed.[4]

In *Conqueror:*
Opened fire on attacking German destroyers—rather like trying to hit snipe with buckshot—last salvo landed in the smoke made by one particular boat, and in the midst of the splash and smoke there appeared to be debris.[16]

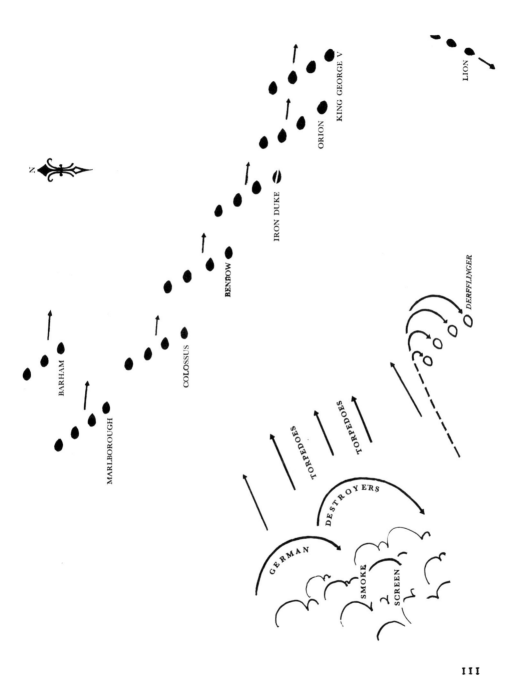

BARHAM

MARLBOROUGH

COLOSSUS

BENBOW

IRON DUKE

ORION

KING GEORGE V

LION

N

DERFFLINGER

TORPEDOES

TORPEDOES

DESTROYERS

GERMAN

SMOKE

SCREEN

III

Another wave of destroyers was approaching and some doubt arose as to whether a two-point turn was sufficient, and a few minutes later the signal was made to turn away another two points—[29]

7.25 P.M.

Jellicoe to Battlefleet and attached cruisers:

Subdivisions separately alter course in succession two points away from Enemy preserving their formation.[4]

Hercules:

I discover through my glasses, in the distance, a slight ruffling of the surface which reminds me of the streaks which extreme cold produces on smooth ice. It is coming towards us from the direction in which the destroyers have just disappeared. I am asked from the fore-top whether I still have the torpedo's track in sight, as they have lost it in the smoke of our last salvoes.[33]

Revenge:

—altered course to port to avoid two torpedoes, one passed about ten yards ahead, the other about twenty yards astern—

Colossus:

—turned to port to avoid a torpedo coming from starboard side—

Barham:

—at least four torpedoes passed through the line close to the *Barham*—[27]

Agincourt:

—aloft the tracks were clearly visible, and acting on the reports from there the ship was gradually turned away, so that by perfect timing one torpedo passed up the port side and one the starboard side—[16]

Collingwood:

—torpedo track was seen 20 degrees abaft the beam and coming straight at the ship; large helm was put on and the torpedo passed very close astern; at the same time another was seen to pass about thirty yards ahead—[27]

Neptune:

—another track was spotted which seemed to be coming straight for us— the bridge then sighted the torpedo and emergency full speed was ordered— from the foretop we were craning our necks over the metal side, while the whole top was groaning and vibrating under the strain of the ship turning at full speed with full helm on—we looked down on the tops of the turrets and the decks below, and could see our shipmates working down there quite unconscious of the immediate peril—the torpedo was now dead astern and coming closer and closer. Nothing happened. The time passed when it should have reached our stern. Still nothing happened. Then somebody laughed, and breaking the spell, we knew that after all it was somehow all right. The miracle was accounted for in *Neptune's* report: "Torpedo was either deflected by the wash from *Neptune's* propellors or ran its range out."[16]

But as the Grand Fleet resumed its southerly course, the enemy battle-line had disappeared. This much the German destroyer thrust had accomplished. Britain had been forced to turn away at a time when Admiral Scheer was in dire emergency, when a little more pressure would have cost him serious loss and perhaps the confusion leading to rout.

Between Britain and the Germans lay clouds of dense black smoke belched from the funnels of the retreating German destroyers.

Jellicoe, certain that Scheer had turned westward, was nevertheless unconscious both of the course on which the invisible High Seas Fleet had attacked and of the unusual nature of the German manœuvre of withdrawal.[22]

All that he had sighted were the dim shapes of a few ships, but whether they were van, centre or rear it was impossible to tell. Now even these had faded away, and whether their vanishing from view was caused by a thickening of the mist or a tactical movement he could only guess. The situation was indeed so completely wrapped in mystery as to baffle even his remarkable powers of penetration.[11]

The German fleet had been extricated from its dangerous contact by the third "swing-around" at 7.17, and the German ships were again safely proceeding on their altered course.

113

One reason for the failure of the British to understand these manœuvres of Admiral Scheer was the fixed conviction of the British that such a simultaneous turn of all the ships of a fleet was impracticable in action—consequently they did not expect it to be used.[19]

von Schoultz in *Hercules:*
It is already beginning to grow dark. Now and again the gunfire weakens, bursting out afresh from time to time. Nothing more is to be seen of the enemy.[33]

Fitfully the firing died away; like a Homeric mist the smother of haze and smoke thickened impenetrably between the combatants, and Admiral Scheer, for the time at least, had saved his fleet; but no more.[11]

The situation was one of extreme peril, for an action the next day might involve the practical annihilation of his fleet. His only hope lay in warding off the British encirclement. If he could reach Horns Reef* by break of day he might still win through and escape the net closing around him. Every four miles he was forced to the westward meant half an hour further from Horns Reef. Admiral Scheer, it must be granted, was a man of quick appreciation and of bold and rapid decision. He decided to make straight for Horns Reef in close order during the night, maintaining his course regardless of attack.[29]

Lieutenant von Leofen at last succeeded at the third attempt in transferring his leader. A second attempt had had to be broken off as the *Moltke* had been in action again. Hipper's flag was run up to her masthead.

On the bridge of his new flagship Hipper did not allow himself much time for his welcome. "We must get to the head of the line." That was his sole concern.

Meanwhile darkness had been falling. The gloomy mist continued to blanket the night. The ships were grey shadows flitting hither and thither. The very silence was full of mystery.[35]

* A group of sandbanks stretching into the North Sea from the Danish peninsula. A channel between them and the mined areas to the west was one of the alternative routes back to Wilhelmshaven.

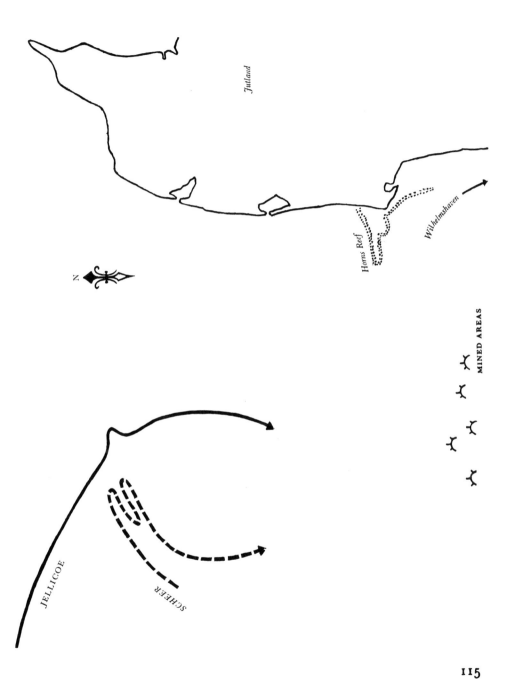

Jutland

Horns Reef

Wilhelmshaven

N

MINED AREAS

JELLICOE

SCHEER

It was just an hour and a half since Jellicoe had deployed the Grand Fleet for battle. During that time his ships had described an enormous semicircle, over twenty miles in diameter, through the sea.

Starting north of the Germans, they had swept round to the east and were now to the south-east . . . Scheer was still within the semicircle, and was being surrounded by an enemy fleet whose numbers were half again as great as his own, whose gun-power was almost double the Germans', and which was gaining a commanding advantage across the German line of escape. One hundred and forty-three British ships were placing themselves between ninety-three German vessels and the German harbours.[22]

"Something tremendous was going on."

Jellicoe decides to avoid a night action, but to keep the British fleet between the Germans and their bases so as to renew the battle at dawn. The Grand Fleet takes up its night formation, with a strong rearguard of light cruisers and destroyers five miles astern of the main body to ward off torpedo attacks.

Scheer orders the High Seas Fleet to steer eastward for home waters, regardless of any British attacks.

During the hours of darkness a series of violent point-blank actions takes place between the light forces of the British rearguard and heavier German ships. Most of the Germans are steering eastward, and some are identified as battleships. The British cruiser Black Prince *is blown up; and several destroyers are disabled, rammed or sunk by gunfire. Among German losses, the light cruiser* Frauenlob *and the battleship* Pommern *are destroyed by torpedoes.*

No word reaches Jellicoe of these clashes, either from the British ships engaged or from battleships at the rear of the main fleet from which gun-flashes and explosions are observed.

At daylight the empty sea makes it apparent that the whole High Seas Fleet has broken through the British rearguard during the night, and has escaped homeward.

Jellicoe's account:

The possibility of a night action was, of course, present to my mind, but for several reasons it was not my intention to seek such an action between the heavy ships.

In the first place, such a course must have inevitably led to our Battle Fleet being the object of attack by a very large destroyer force throughout the night.

It was known to me that neither our searchlights nor their control arrangements were at this time of the best type. The fitting of Director-Firing gear for the guns of the secondary armament of our battleships (a very important factor for firing at night) had also only just begun, although repeatedly applied for.

The result of night actions between heavy ships must always be very largely a matter of *chance*, as there is little opportunity for skill on either side. It is, therefore, an undesirable procedure on these general grounds.

The question then remained as to the course to be steered. The first desideratum was to keep the British fleet between the enemy and his bases, so as to be in a position to renew the action at dawn. I considered that a southerly course would meet the situation.[26]

Scheer:

If we could succeed in warding off the enemy's encircling movement, and could be the first to reach Horns Reef, then the liberty of decision for the next morning was assured to us. The Main Fleet in close formation was to make for Horns Reef by the shortest route, and, defying all enemy attacks, keep on that course.[32]

9.10 P.M.

Scheer to High Seas Fleet:

Gros Kurs SSO¼O durchhalten. Fahrt 16 Seemeilen. Grosse Kreuzer anhängen.[23]

Fleet must maintain course SSE¼E. Speed 16 knots. Battle-cruisers join astern.

At 9.17 Jellicoe ordered the Grand Fleet to take up night-cruising formation and to hold to the south at 17 knots. The battleships, answering the command, closed up into three columns abreast, distance between the columns one mile.

Directly ahead of the main body, the Fourth Light Cruiser Squadron took up scouting station five miles in the van, to guard against frontal attacks. Five miles in the rear, the flotillas of destroyers were distributed as a rear-guard—58 torpedo-craft to protect the hind-quarters of the fleet from attacks by enemy light craft, and to keep watch lest the German battle fleet should strike down astern.[22]

The Admiralty had intercepted and deciphered certain of the German signals:

9.55 P.M.
Admiralty to Jellicoe:
Three destroyer flotillas have been ordered to attack you during the night.

9.58 P.M.
Admiralty to Jellicoe:
At 9 p.m. rear ship of enemy Battlefleet in Lat. 56 33′ N., Long. 5° 30′ E.[4]

This message placed the rear German battleship ten miles south west of *Iron Duke*. Jellicoe knew that this was wrong. At 9 p.m. the German fleet bore north west from him.

Dreyer in *Iron Duke*:
During the night, in view of the close proximity of heavy enemy ships, the hands remained at action stations, the crews at their guns, but being allowed to sleep in turn. Corned beef and biscuits were served out at the quarters. Cocoa was provided at 9.30 p.m. and onwards.

Jellicoe lay down for a few hours in his clothes on a settee in the small house on the bridge, known as the Admiral's shelter, in which his tactical plot was kept.[13]

The fates were busy, weaving the threads of destiny. The blind fleets, unconscious of the workings of circumstance, steamed almost side by side, so close to each other in the darkness that they were like members of one great common formation.

Their courses were slightly converging . . .

And the episodes of the night, which cost blood and ships on both sides, centred about the clashes which took place as the German van and the British flotillas stumbled into each other in the dark, holding to their courses, unaware that they were crossing pathways, each believing the other was attacking.[22]

Navigating Officer of *Nottingham* (2nd Light Cruiser Squadron):
I had been on the bridge since 2 p.m. with no extra clothing on, and I don't

think that I had ever felt so cold before, but one cannot send people down to one's cabin to fetch overcoats in the middle of the Battle of Jutland. It was a relief now to get into a greatcoat and to sit down on the bridge for a few minutes and munch a sandwich.

All was quiet for a time, and we kept undisturbed on our course until—[16]

King-Hall in *Southampton* (2nd Light Cruiser Squadron):

—a signalman, and Ireland, the navigator, suddenly whispered: "Five ships on the beam."

From their faint silhouettes it was impossible to discover more than that they were light cruisers. I decided to go aft as quickly as possible. On the way aft I looked in at the after-control, where Haworth-Booth said to me: "There are five Huns on the beam. What on earth is going on?"

We began to challenge with our obsolete system whilst the Germans switched on coloured lights at their fore yardarms.

A second later a solitary gun crashed forth from the *Dublin*, the ship next astern of us. Simultaneously I saw the shell hit a ship just above the waterline and about 800 yards away. As I caught a nightmare-like glimpse of her interior, I said to myself, "My God, they are alongside us."

At that moment the Germans switched on their searchlights, and we switched on ours. Before I was blinded by the lights in my eyes I caught sight of a line of light-grey ships. Then the gun behind which I was standing answered my shout of ''Fire!''

The action lasted three and a half minutes.

The range was so close that the German shots went high, just high enough to burst on the upper deck and around the after superstructure and bridge. And in a light cruiser that's where all the flesh and blood stands to battle.

One shell had burst on the side just below the gun, and the fragments had whipped over the top of the low bulwark and mown the men down.

Another shell had burst on the searchlight just above us. The fragments from this shell descended upon the waist like hail, and scoured out the insides of the gun-shields of the two 6-inch guns, manned by marines, one gun each side.

And then I was standing in a fire. The flash of some exploding shell had ignited half a dozen rounds of cordite.

120

Two pillars of white flame rose splendidly aloft. One roared up the foremast, the other reached above the tops of the second and third funnels.

This then was the end. There could be no doubt; the central ammunition hoist was between those two funnels.

What was it going to feel like to blow up?

Let me see—how had the *Queen Mary* looked?

Fascinating sight, those two pillars of white flame.

By heaven, the centre one had turned red, it wavered, it decreased in height; it grew again, but the spell was broken, and I rushed to the ladder which led from the waist to the boat-deck in order to get up to the fire and assist. I ran a few steps and tripped over a heap of bodies. I got up, tried not to tread on soft things, and arrived on the boat-deck.

The firing had ceased, the Commander and the Sub were at the central fire. It suddenly went out, so did the foremost one.

Everything was pitch black.

Where were the Germans?

Nothing but groans from dark corners.

Though I did not know it at the time, the Germans had fled.

They fled because Allen, our Torpedo-Lieutenant, had fired a 21-inch torpedo. At forty-one knots the torpedo had shot across and, striking the *Frauenlob*, had blown her in half.[24]

The flicker of gun-fire, the glare of distant searchlights, were seen from the dreadnoughts at the rear of the British main body. Their significance was misunderstood—they were interpreted to mean that enemy torpedo craft were endeavouring to attack from astern and were being beaten off by the destroyers stationed there for that purpose. The episode was not considered important enough to report to the Fleet Flagship.[22]

Meanwhile the Admiralty had deciphered Scheer's signal of 9.10 p.m. to the High Seas Fleet. Other signals from him had also been intercepted, including one requesting airship reconnaissance over the Horns Reef area at dawn. This, if passed to Jellicoe, would have given him a strong indication of Scheer's intended route home. Instead:

10.41 P.M.

Admiralty to Jellicoe:

> German Battle Fleet ordered home at 9.14 p.m. Battle-cruisers in rear. Course S.S.E. ¾ E. Speed 16 knots.[4]

The enemy course and speed, as established by the Admiralty, pointed to Horns Reef as the German goal, but Jellicoe's confidence in the infallibility of Admiralty intelligence had been shaken, and he felt it inadvisable to stake everything upon this one message. Here at sea there was an entire lack of evidence to confirm the Admiralty's information. It seemed impossible that the enemy's fleet, on this course, could come barging into some part of the Grand Fleet's huge formation without messages pouring into the Fleet Flagship to tell of the contact.

Throughout the night no messages came.[22]

A destroyer officer:

We couldn't tell what was happening. Every now and then out of the silence would come *bang, bang, boom*, as hard as it could go for ten minutes on end. The flash of the guns lit up the whole sky for miles and miles, and the noise was far more penetrating than by day. Then you would see a great burst of flame from some poor devil, as the searchlights switched on and off, and then perfect silence once more.[7]

11.30 P.M.

> The van of the High Seas Fleet breaks through the destroyers of the British 4th Flotilla.

Broke's narrative:

The outlines of three ships were made out on the starboard beam, steaming in the same direction as ourselves. *Tipperary* was seen to make the challenge, but it was answered by the simultaneous switching on of searchlights in all three ships.

Almost simultaneously a heavy and accurate fire was directed on *Tipperary*. Splashes of the shells striking the water all around her could be seen, and in what appeared to be less than a minute she burst into flames.[16]

Spitfire's narrative:

We closed the *Tipperary*, now a mass of burning wreckage. As we neared we saw a German cruiser. Suddenly the Captain realised that she had seen us, and was trying to ram us. She was coming at us full speed across our port bow. The Captain ordered "Hard-a-starboard: full speed ahead both," and, leaning over the bridge screen, shouted "Clear the foc'sle." It wasn't a minute too soon, as with an awful crash the two ships met end on, port bow to port bow. As we bumped, the enemy opened fire with their foc'sle guns. Our foremast came tumbling down, our for'ard searchlight found its way from its platform above the fore-bridge down to the deck, and the foremost funnel was blown back till it rested neatly between the two foremost ventilation cowls, like the hinging funnel of a penny river steamboat. The enemy surged down our port side clearing everything before her; the boats came crashing down and even the davits were torn out of their sockets, and all the time she was firing her guns just over our heads.[16]

Broke's narrative:

The hull of a large ship was sighted on the starboard bow.* The Captain immediately gave the order to challenge, but almost as he spoke the stranger switched on a vertical string of coloured lights, an unknown signal in our service.

"Starboard 20; full speed both; starboard foremost tube fire when your sights come on; all guns—Green 40—a battleship" . . . but the German had evidently been watching our movements, and we were too late.

He switched on a blaze of searchlights straight into our eyes, and so great was the dazzling effect that it made us feel quite helpless. Then after another interval of about a second, shells could be heard screaming over our heads. Shouting to the Captain that I was going below, I jumped down on to the lower bridge. There, in the darkness, I found complete chaos. The quartermaster and telegrapher were both killed, and the wheel and telegraphs were shattered . . . just starting to strike matches to make certain that communication with the engine-room was gone, when I heard the Captain's voice down the pipe shouting "Full speed astern both."

I looked up for an instant and saw a green bow light of some other ship just ahead of us—[16]

*It was *Westfalen*, leading the German battleship line.

Sparrowhawk's narrative:

—we saw the *Broke* coming straight for our bridge, absolutely end on, at 28 knots. I clean forgot all about the Germans and their gunfire . . . but as she hit us I remember shouting out "Now!" and then nothing more till I found myself lying on the foc'sle, not of our ship, but of the *Broke*. The whole of the *Broke's* foc'sle was an absolute shambles, but I crawled along until I came to a place where I could stand up. There was a perishing noise going on all the time, as the Germans were still endeavouring to sink the ship. As I was getting to my feet I met a fellow, who said "Who the hell are you?" I told him I was the sub-lieutenant of the *Sparrowhawk*, and that I was going to report to the Captain of the *Broke* and ask for a job. He told me that the Captain was on the remains of the bridge, and disappeared.[16]

This action was seen from at least two battleships at the rear of the British main fleet.

Report of the Captain of *Valiant*:

At 11.35 p.m. observed heavy firing on starboard quarter. From the evidence we surmised that there appeared to be two German cruisers with at least two funnels and a crane amidships, apparently steering to the eastward at a high speed. These cruisers then evidently sighted an unknown small number of British ships ahead of them, possibly a light cruiser and a few destroyers. Both Germans switched on top searchlights and opened a very rapid and extraordinarily accurate independent fire on our light cruiser. She replied, but was soon in flames fore and aft. The enemy, after five minutes, ceased fire and switched off.[4]

Report of the Captain of *Malaya*:

11.40. Three points abaft starboard beam observed what appeared to be an attack by our destroyers on some enemy big ships steering the same way as ours, two of which used searchlights. One of our destroyers, with three funnels (appearance of *Termagant* class), was set on fire, but not before she had hit the second ship. This was seen by the column of smoke, and also the explosion was distinctly heard and felt.

The leading ship of the enemy, which was seen by the flash of the explosion, had two masts, two funnels, and a conspicuous crane (apparently *Westfalen* class).[4]

124

—the uncertainty, the continuous strain of looking out, the anxiety to know if a ship is friend or foe, the responsibility of opening fire, the completely blinding effect of light in one's eyes after a long darkness—[16]

Destroyers of the British 4th Flotilla encounter the High Seas Fleet again.

Ardent's narrative:
I clearly perceived four big ships on a nearly parallel but slightly converging course. They challenged several times, and their challenge was not an English one. They then switched on their searchlights, picked up the *Fortune*, and opened fire on her. I could see the *Fortune* was hard hit, so altered round to starboard and fired a torpedo at the leading enemy ship. We could all see it hit, and there was an enormous upheaval of water right forward. We caught a last glimpse of the *Fortune*, on fire and in a sinking condition, but fighting still.

Smoke was reported right ahead ... a big ship steaming on exactly the opposite course to us. I attacked at once, and from a very close range our remaining torpedoes were fired, but before I could judge of the effect the enemy switched on searchlights and found us at once. I then became aware that the *Ardent* was taking on a division of German battleships. Our guns were useless against such big adversaries; our torpedoes were fired; we could do no more, but wait in the full glare of the blinding searchlights for the shells. It must only have been seconds, but it seemed like hours. At last it came, and as the first salvo hit I heard a seaman ejaculate "Oo-ooh," as one does to a bursting rocket. Shell after shell hit us, and our speed diminished and then stopped; then the dynamo stopped, and all the lights went out. I could feel the ship was sinking.[16]

ABOUT MIDNIGHT
Scheer to High Seas Fleet:
Durchhalten.[23]
Hold the course.

12.10 A.M.
A solitary British ship was coming south through the darkness—the old

armoured cruiser *Black Prince*, which had become separated from her consorts and had steamed after the Grand Fleet for hours, hoping to rejoin.

Dreadnoughts in the west . . . surely these were her friends.

She drew closer . . . confidently flashed the recognition signal.

Her answer came from the guns of *Thüringen, Ostfriesland* and *Friedrich der Grosse*—a tornado of turret-shell at point-blank range.

The unfortunate armoured cruiser was never able to open fire in reply. Roaring like an incandescent furnace, she drove past the full length of the German line, two of her four funnels blown overboard, lurid yellow-red flames shooting a hundred feet high out of her, a few men running on her deck, her metal glowing red with the heat. Out of control she passed within yards of the drifting *Spitfire*, lighting the Stygian darkness until, with an explosion like a thunder-clap, she and every man of her crew disappeared beneath the sea.[22]

An officer in the battleship *Canada*:

Something tremendous was going on only a few miles away, but to our astonishment the Battle Fleet continued to steam to the southward.[5]

12.25 A.M.

Again the German line cuts through British destroyers.

Nicator's narrative:

Suddenly we saw challenging going on, and some ship, I do not know which, switched on its fighting lights for a second or two and then off again, apparently by accident. Then without any warning searchlights were switched on abaft our starboard beam, and settled on the *Petard*, ahead of us. We saw three or four big ships, obviously Germans, silhouetted for a moment; then a burst of fire, followed quickly by another, and the lights went out. The *Petard* was badly hit, and suffered a lot of casualties. Then all lights switched on again, this time on us for a fraction of a minute during which time we thought we were in for it too, but they trained aft on to the *Turbulent*, two ships astern of us. She appeared to be at absolutely point-blank range, and in a few seconds a ripple of fire seemed to run the whole length of her.

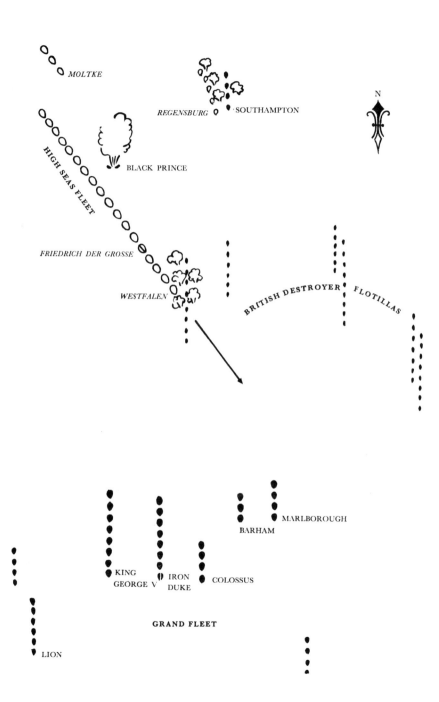

MOLTKE

REGENSBURG   SOUTHAMPTON

N

HIGH SEAS FLEET

BLACK PRINCE

FRIEDRICH DER GROSSE

WESTFALEN

BRITISH DESTROYER FLOTILLAS

KING
GEORGE V

IRON
DUKE

COLOSSUS

BARHAM

MARLBOROUGH

GRAND FLEET

LION

It looked as if she were blown right out of the water. It all happened so suddenly that we hardly realised what was taking place, and it somehow did not strike us that this was the German fleet breaking through the line, unluckily at the weakest point.[16]

For a long time, more than an hour, there was silence—the silence of deep night—so that the watching, waiting men found themselves struggling with the almost overpowering desire to sleep.[22]

In the darkness lay Hipper's shattered flagship *Lützow*. Captain von Harder describes her end:

After it became clear that it was not possible to save the ship, because she had 8,300 tons of water in her and was on the point of heeling over, I decided to send off the crew so as to save them from disaster. I got them all, the wounded included, into the destroyers which had come alongside. Many cheers were given for His Majesty the Kaiser, our leaders Scheer and Hipper and the good ship herself. She was so down by the bows that the water came up to the control tower and the stern was right out. On my orders the ship was sunk by a torpedo fired by G 38. She heeled over and after two minutes swiftly sank with her flag flying.[36]

1.43 A.M.

Once more Scheer's battleships cross the path of British destroyers—this time the 12th Flotilla, led by *Faulknor*.

Obedient's narrative:

As daylight was appearing, a line of ships were sighted on the starboard beam. Owing to the mist we could not at once determine whether they were enemy ships or not, but our doubts were very soon dispelled by one of them challenging us. She flashed the letter " K " in morse code, but this was not the correct challenge for the night, so obviously the ships were Germans. We were the division nearest to the enemy, and at first we thought that *Faulknor* was not aware of them, and so ran alongside to tell him of them by megaphone.[16]

1.52 A.M.

Faulknor to Jellicoe:

URGENT. PRIORITY.

Enemy's battlefleet steering S.E. approximate bearing S.W. My position ten miles astern of First Battle Squadron.

URGENT.

I am attacking.[29]

Jellicoe's report:

This signal was unfortunately not received in the battle fleet owing to telefunken interference.[4]

Faulknor's narrative:

At two minutes past 2 the *Faulknor* fired her first torpedo, which probably passed ahead of the second enemy ship.

About two minutes later the second torpedo was fired, but almost simultaneously with this the Germans sighted our flotilla and all their battleships opened fire, together with the light cruisers astern of their line. The sea seemed to be alive with bursting shells and the air with the whistle of passing projectiles. Suddenly a huge explosion took place in the third German ship—[16]

Obedient's narrative:

—on the waterline of the ship—the *Pommern*—appeared a dull red ball of fire. Quicker than one can imagine it spread fore and aft, until reaching the foremast and mainmast it flared upwards, up the masts in big red tongues of flame, uniting between the mastheads in a big, black cloud of smoke and sparks. Then one saw the ends of the ship come up as though her back was broken, before the mist shut her out from view. In the silence that followed, a voice on our bridge was heard to say " Pity the poor devils, they ain't drawn their month's money."[16]

And while the wild scenes of din and glare, of fire and destruction, had been enacting themselves within sight of the near British battle squadrons, no tidings of their progress or details of the forces engaged reached the *Iron Duke*.

In his shelter, Jellicoe lay resting, undisturbed, as the opportunity for the most decisive victory in naval history slipped through his fingers.[28]

The crippled cruiser *Warrior* was limping homeward, towed by the seaplane-carrier *Engadine*.

In *Warrior:*

All through the night we struggled on, trying to keep pace with the water by strenuous exertion all round. About midnight we all met in the ward-room, where the messman had managed to produce a ham and a loaf or two of bread. I mumbled a few pieces of dry bread in a dry mouth, but I couldn't go on with it. And the only thing we could find to drink was one bottle of port.

I realised that she was rapidly losing her stability, and by the way the water was rising, I knew she could not last much longer. When I went up to report my opinion to the Captain, I found that he had just come to the same conclusion, and at that very moment the Commander came up and made the same announcement. Consequently the skipper waited no longer, but signalled to the *Engadine* to cast off the tow and come alongside.[16]

In *Engadine*:

The sea was bad: the little *Engadine* bobbed about like a cork, and the *Warrior* was moving in every direction as if she was loth to give up the fight, but knew that she was doomed. Her crew were fallen in on her deck, well back from the ship's side against the funnel casing, looking as indifferent to their danger as men possibly can.

The risk of *Engadine* going alongside *Warrior* to take off the crew was tremendous, but there was no hesitation on the part of the Captain, and the crew were with him to a man. The starboard side of *Warrior* was tried first, but looked too bad: so the port side was then tried, but it looked worse. The *Engadine* then lay off the starboard quarter of *Warrior*, which must have taxed the nerves of the *Warrior's* crew to the uttermost seeing, after all they had gone through, that apparently they had now either to swim through this seaway to the *Engadine* or else go down with the ship. Those that had collected pieces of enemy shells as souvenirs quietly placed them on one side, in order that they might have less weight to carry on their swim.

The *Engadine*, however, was only waiting for the *Warrior's* yawing from side to side to steady a little before attempting to get alongside her again on the starboard side. After a few minutes, which must have seemed hours to the *Warrior's* men, the *Engadine* was placed alongside, in a manner which I think was agreed by all to be a wonderful piece of seamanship. The ships were made fast together, but worked against each other most viciously; yet all the *Warrior's* men remained steady waiting their Captain's order to abandon ship. Then the Captain gave the order, and things moved. Each man's ration of bully beef and bread was hurled on board us, and one large mass of men poured over the nettings into the ship.

At this moment the Captain considered that there was too much haste, and he ordered the bugle "Still" to be sounded. The result was wonderful. Not a single man passed from the *Warrior* to the *Engadine* after this bugle was sounded, but every man fell back from the ship's side against the funnel casing.

When the "Carry On" was sounded, all those still left in the *Warrior* hastened to abandon ship. The wounded were got across—[16]

Captain of *Engadine*:

—in transferring the wounded, owing to the motion between the ships, one man slipped off a stretcher and fell between the two ships. The Captain of the *Warrior*, who was on the bridge, gave the order that no one was to go over after him as it appeared certain that whoever went must be crushed to death immediately; but Flight-Lieutenant Rutland of my ship climbed over forward unseen, and reached the man at great risk to himself, for which gallant act he afterwards received the Albert Medal.

When all were on board we got clear of the *Warrior* without difficulty. She looked a sad sight lying there derelict and deserted, and it was obvious that she would not keep afloat very much longer.[16]

Sparrowhawk, helpless after her collision with *Broke*, drifted through the night. A German destroyer stopped within a hundred yards of her and, without firing a shot, gathered way again and disappeared. Then:

Out of the misty half-light of the morning a dim shape approached, which with despair was recognised to be that of one of the latest German light cruisers, and the *Sparrowhawks* again prepared for their end. But their course was not yet run. The light cruiser started to heel over to one side, to settle down forward, then quietly stood on her head, and—sank.[15]

The enemy meanwhile had swept right across the stern of the fleet during the night. At dawn his ships were still 16 miles from Horns Reef and scores of glasses swept the horizon anxiously for the British fleet which they fully expected to see. To their surprise and intense relief it was not there.[29]

Commander Bingham, whose ship *Nestor* had been sunk the day before, was now a prisoner on board the German destroyer S 15:

Lying on top of the Captain's bunk in semi-darkness, with clothes slowly drying on me, weary and feeling that one had reached the end, no wonder if I began to reflect about the immediate future. How was it all going to end? Assuming the British sank this German T.B.D. should we pull through, after a scuffle with the sentry, another bath in the North Sea, and with the remote chance of being picked up by a British destroyer in the dark? Probably not. On the other hand, if the German destroyer came through unscathed, one would emerge from the business with a whole skin, with a certainty of a dreary spell of captivity, but with the hope of serving under the White Ensign at a future date.

The long-drawn torture of this ghastly night crept on until the first tinge of dawn found its way into the cabin.

The sub-lieutenant of the destroyer came below, and after ordering some breakfast for us, announced that the battle was over and that the destroyer was shaping course for Wilhelmshaven.

It was only natural to ask him which side had gained the victory. He simply said "I", and pointed to his chest.[6]

In *Neptune*:

I got down from the top for a spell. There was an awful litter of stuff everywhere between decks, chiefly made by the shock of our broadsides dislodging loosely stowed gear. I found the gunnery lieutenant gazing into his cabin, speechless, for the electric radiator had been overwhelmed by the tin bath landing on it from above, all the drawers had shaken out, and his clothes were a melee on the floor with much other odd matter. Moreover, the fire brigade party, zealous to guard against the chance of the cabin catching fire, had played their hose into the midst, thoughtfully filling the bath at the same time.[16]

In *Lion*:

Between decks everything was in total darkness, and the atmosphere was thick with cordite fumes, blending disagreeably with the smell of burnt paint, burnt flesh, and chloroform. I groped my way along the mess decks and narrowly escaped falling down several great yawning chasms in the deck—places where shells had burst. Finally I observed a lighted room, and thought "Thank Heaven, here is the ward-room and food at last," but it was actually the Captain's cabin, which the Fleet Surgeon was using as an operating theatre.[16]

In *Southampton*:

The dressing station was an ill-ventilated bathroom situated just over the boiler-rooms. An operating table was in the middle, and the deck as well as the passage outside was a litter of mangled men laid out in rows by the first-aid parties. Add to this a foul atmosphere thick with chloroform, and the painfully depressing sight of numbers of badly wounded men waiting their turn for attention.

As each case was passed through the doctor's hands and his wounds were dressed he was removed to the ward-room, though this soon became over-crowded, and all officers' cabins were requisitioned. Several cabins were wrecked, and there was a good deal of water about dripping through from the deck above, where fire mains were burst.[16]

So at 2.47 a.m. on June 1st the Battle Fleet turned to the north, sent out the light forces ahead and on the wings to gain touch with the enemy, and the crews of the fleet, though tired after the strained watching and waiting of the night, closed up with eagerness at their action stations, making all those little final preparations which one makes when the moment of the test approaches. But there was to be no test. June 1st was to bring only a maturing disappointment. As no reports came from the scouts spread ahead, as nothing but the familiar silhouettes of our own ships could be seen on either hand, gradually it was borne home to the British fleet that the Battle of Jutland was finished. The scouting forces could find no enemy ships about, no sign of the

German battle fleet, for the German battle fleet were past them, to the eastward of them, making their way down the swept channel off Schleswig Holstein.[15]

In *Neptune*:

About 3 a.m. a Zeppelin suddenly appeared out of the morning haze and steered towards us until the ensign trailing from its car could be seen. I had never seen a Zeppelin before, and regarded it curiously. An order was passed to "X" turret to fire one round at it at maximum elevation. Our next ahead fired a whole salvo, and other ships started in. Our round went off, and for a brief second I could see the projectile in the air, but then the airship lifted its nose disdainfully to the morning breeze and disappeared, and a signal was received ordering us not to waste ammunition. Not until the Zeppelin was out of sight did I realise the full significance of this early morning visit. It meant that the Germans now knew exactly where we were; we should not see the High Seas Fleet that day.[16]

Captain von Egidy gets the crippled *Seydlitz* home:

The navigation apparatus had suffered severely during the action, the charts were partially obliterated by the blood of men who had fallen in the control tower. Only the hand steering machine was available for steering. The result was that just before we reached Horns Reef the ship grounded slightly twice and had to be got off by reversing the engines. *Pillau* stood by to protect the much-tried battle-cruiser.

While we were passing through the Amrum Bank the ship gradually settled deeper and deeper. Yet at times we actually had to increase speed to force a way through shallow passages where the keel was sliding along the bottom. The business of baling with buckets which had to be kept up in devastated, ill-lit rooms filled with jagged fragments and (in many cases) human remains, placed an extreme strain on the men. In all we had 5300 tons of water aboard.

Two pumping ships from ashore came alongside. They made fast, began to pump and simultaneously helped the wounded giant by using their engines to increase the effect of the rudder. A tedious but extremely skilful piece of handling got her to Wilhelmshaven at last.[36]

The British fleet swept up and down over their track of the night and over the area of yesterday's fleet action until 1.15 p.m., but no enemy ships were to be found. There were relics of the fight. Patches of oil, with in the centre some wreckage or even the bows of a ship still sticking up, and floating bodies around. It was even possible in a very few cases to rescue a man here or there still alive, but very few of these, for the cold of the North Sea waters is soon numbing in its effect, and humans floating in it mercifully soon lose their senses, become drowsy, and then drown.[15]

The Captain of *Ardent*:
I found a skiff's oar floating past, and put it under my arms. I began to feel very drowsy, and dropped off into a sort of sleep several times, only to be awakened again by waves slapping into my face. Once more I woke to find a flotilla leader—the *Marksman*—close alongside me. I sang out for help.[16]

In *Marksman*:
We observed and picked up two raft-loads of the *Fortune's* men, including their chief artificer engineer. The whole sea for a large distance round was a mass of oil, and it was also in this area that we came upon the Captain of the *Ardent*, who had been in the water some five hours, and was in the last stages of exhaustion.[16]

In *Dublin*:
We passed through large quantities of floating wreckage, hammocks, bodies, etc. An alert signalman reported he saw a hand waving from a spar some distance away, and on closing we were fortunately able to rescue a stoker belonging to the *Tipperary*, who informed us that his ship had been sunk some four or five hours previously.[16]

In *New Zealand*:
The only signs of the enemy were hundreds of their drowned blue-jackets in their life-saving waistcoats, floating near the great smears of oil and wreckage that marked the grave of some ship, with also large numbers of dead fish, apparently killed by the explosion.[16]

135

In *Spitfire*:

We held a funeral service for the men who had been killed. In accordance with the custom, they were lashed up in their hammocks, with a practice projectile at their head and feet, and laid on the quarter deck. Volunteers acted as bearers, and the Captain read the funeral service. The colours under which they had fought were half-masted, and we lowered their bodies as reverently as we could into the deep; there was a big sea running.[16]

In *Lion*:

In the afternoon Beatty came into the *Lion's* chart-house. Tired and depressed, he sat down on the settee, and settling himself in a corner he closed his eyes. Unable to hide his disappointment at the result of the battle, he repeated in a weary voice, "There is something wrong with our ships," then opening his eyes he added, "And something wrong with our system." Having thus unburdened himself he fell asleep.[8]

The Reckoning

London, 3 June 1916.

The Secretary of the Admiralty makes the following announcement:

On the afternoon of Wednesday, May 31st, a naval engagement took place off the coast of Jutland.

The British ships on which the brunt of the fighting fell were the Battle Cruiser Fleet and some cruisers and light cruisers supported by four fast battleships. Among these the losses were heavy.

The German Battle Fleet, aided by low visibility, avoided prolonged action with our main forces, and soon after these appeared on the scene the enemy returned to port, though not before receiving severe damage from our battleships.

The battle cruisers *Queen Mary, Indefatigable, Invincible,* and the cruisers *Defence* and *Black Prince* were sunk. The *Warrior* was disabled, and after being towed for some time had to be abandoned by her crew.

It is also known that the destroyers *Tipperary, Turbulent, Fortune, Sparrow-hawk* and *Ardent* were lost, and six others are not yet accounted for.

No British battleships or light cruisers were sunk.

The enemy's losses were serious.

At least one battle cruiser was destroyed, and one severely damaged; one battleship reported sunk by our destroyers during a night attack; two light cruisers were disabled and probably sunk.

The exact number of enemy destroyers disposed of during the action cannot be ascertained with any certainty, but it must have been large.

Wilhelmshaven, 5 June 1916.

The Kaiser addresses the crews of the High Seas Fleet:

The gigantic fleet of Albion, ruler of the seas, which, since Trafalgar, for a hundred years has imposed on the whole world a bond of sea tyranny, and has surrounded itself with a nimbus of invincibleness, came into the field. That gigantic armada approached, and our fleet engaged it. The British fleet was beaten. The first great hammer blow was struck, and the nimbus of British world supremacy disappeared.

The two statements, British and German, made immediately after the battle accurately reflect the states of mind that Jutland produced in the nations which fought it. The Admiralty communique is pessimistically exact in reporting British losses; vague as regards damage inflicted on the enemy. It leaves an impression of being drafted to conceal a disaster. The Kaiser's speech boldly claims a victory so triumphant that details would seem superfluous.

To Germany, the battle brought at least three benefits. The first was a tremendous psychological boost, at home and abroad. The High Seas Fleet, developed in only sixteen years, had proved itself able to face the full might and tradition of British seapower and survive. Second, the fact that the German fleet remained a powerful force closed the entry to the Baltic to Allied shipping. No promise could now be held out to the Russians of supplies for their desperately ill-equipped armies; and to that extent Jutland was a factor in the removal of Russia from the war. Third, it provided strong evidence to support the conviction of the German naval realists that their future in sea warfare lay not on the surface but beneath it. Despite all his precautions Scheer had met the full strength of the Grand Fleet; and he knew now that his chances of avoiding superior British numbers henceforth were smaller still. "A victorious termination of the war within measurable time," he reported to the Kaiser, "can only be obtained by destroying the economic resources of Great Britain, namely, by the employment of submarines against British commerce." This argument had been advanced before, but the Kaiser had demurred on the grounds of its adverse effect on American opinion. After the hairbreadth escape of his beloved fleet at Jutland, and in view of the enhanced prestige of the Imperial Navy as a result of the battle, he no longer opposed it; and unrestricted U-boat warfare followed. In this context, the British claim that Jutland sealed up the High Seas Fleet in its home ports for the rest of the war overlooks the fact that its presence kept the U-boat bases open. The German surface fleet in being made the U-boat campaigns possible; and the U-boats set the direction of Germany's naval endeavour for the next thirty years. That Scheer was correct needs little argument: by those on both sides of the ocean who fought it, the outcome of the Battle of the Atlantic was hardly considered a foregone conclusion.

In the wider term, the influence of Jutland was more ominous for Germany. If it helped to take Tzarist Russia out of the war, it presumably assisted the advent of the Bolsheviks to power. And if the U-boats which it unleashed came close to success, they, and later the Soviet ascendency, were instrumental in bringing America not only into the First World War, but into the destinies of Europe and the high seas. Thus that thunderous day and night in the North Sea were one of the visible hinges closing the door of history on the nineteenth century patterns of power, and opening it to those of the twentieth.

For Britain, Jutland was a shocking blow. Within hours, rumours of a major defeat were so strong that dockyard workers booed damaged ships as they returned to base with their dead and wounded still on board. And as more balanced information came to light and the frustrating indecisiveness of the battle emerged, a controversy began to divide naval circles. This dispute, originating over the tactics of the battle, came to revolve around the parts played respectively by Jellicoe and Beatty. To one school, Beatty was the hero of the day. In his verve and aggressiveness as a fighting commander, in his sense of his ships and his faith in his men, he showed the spirit of Nelson; and if the Grand Fleet as a whole, and not merely the battle-cruisers, had been in his hands, the issue would not have been in doubt. To this school, Jellicoe was a technician and an administrator; and on *Iron Duke's* bridge he could only act by the insipid dogma of the rule-book. He deployed on the wrong column. Or he should not have deployed at all, but should have launched his squadrons independently to break the German line into chaos. He was over-cautious; his leadership was prim and even pompous; he was unsuited to the supreme command. To the other camp, Beatty's actions were rash to the point of folly. He was roundly defeated by Hipper; and his remaining ships were only saved by the 5th Battle Squadron after he had first left it behind in his impetuous initial attack on the German battle-cruisers, and then allowed it to face the whole High Seas Fleet alone when he himself turned to the north. Jellicoe's handling of the main fleet, by contrast, showed the qualities of a mature commander. His masterly tactics in effect won the battle; and if he could not drive home the advantage he had so ably gained, it was largely due to the lack of accurate information reaching him from his subordinates, including and especially Beatty.

The matter of the dispute was not new; it was a continuation with new evidence of the debate which, in word or action, had been with the Navy for nearly two centuries. More significant was its manner: its duration (it is not dead even today), and the violence with which it was conducted. These suggest that it was more than an airing of conflicting naval opinion; rather, that it was a vent for deeply wounded professional and national pride, a rationalisation of the stark fact that Jutland had extinguished the Trafalgar legacy. At 4.30 in the afternoon of 21 October 1805, with Villeneuve's ships shattered, captured or running for safety, an assumption had been born. Accepted by Britain and, by and large, by other maritime nations, it was that to challenge British seapower meant defeat. On 1 June 1916, when the breaking dawn revealed the empty North Sea, the assumption had ceased to be valid. And the controversy that followed was, in part, the search for a scapegoat.

It is possible that in the circumstances of 1916 an outcome resembling that of Trafalgar was so unlikely that it would have been wise to prepare public opinion in advance for a disappointment. In 1805, all the factors inherent in naval combat—ships, guns, crews, wind—were matters of knowledge reinforced by constant practical experience. By 1914 the nature of sea warfare had undergone changes almost as complete as that from the arrow to the atom bomb. The effects of these changes, until they could be measured in action, could only be the subject of informed guesses; and the century of maritime peace had prevented measurement. At Jutland, for example, the new submarine threat was greatly over-estimated. Time and again ships' reports refer to periscopes sighted, oil patches observed, submerged obstructions rammed. Just after *Marlborough* was damaged by a torpedo, *Revenge* was sure that she had "struck and sunk the submarine." Yet no submarines, British or German, were present in the battle area; and the torpedo fired at *Marlborough* certainly came from a surface ship, and probably from the crippled *Wiesbaden*. For such reasons the first full trial of naval strength based on industrial technology was perhaps bound to be experimental. The new navies, with only such guiding evidence as could be gleaned from Togo's defeat of the Russian fleet at Tsushima, were feeling their way into the warfare of metallurgy and chemistry. And because such vast expenditure of money and effort had gone into their building, the first test was likely to be tentative.

Thus Beatty and Hipper were in a different category to Jellicoe and Scheer. They had met before at the Dogger Bank, and had some measure of each other's mettle. And their battle-cruiser forces, forming only a small part of the respective fleets, were ultimately expendable. They could afford to take chances, push their ships to the limit as modern fighting machines, create around themselves the image of being the dashing cavalry commanders of the sea. Jellicoe and Scheer could not. The huge battleship fleets in their hands represented, in Scheer's case the expression of a national will; in Jellicoe's the insurance of an empire. Both were highly competent seamen: but their roles at Jutland required them to be less seamen than seagoing trustees. Jellicoe is an imperturbable intellectual. He knows precisely from prior reasoning the limits within which he can operate. Nothing can cause him to step outside them. Even at the moment of the most fearful test of nerve a man could well undergo, his calm and politeness are unshakeable. He can accept his isolation because he does not need the support of others. His background has made him the perfect Senior Prefect, totally loyal to the headmaster's ideas; now he is the perfect servant of state policy. Perhaps his one tactical act open to serious question was his command to turn away from Scheer's torpedoes; and much of the criticism of him hinges round this order. It is pointed out that in the prevailing conditions of mist and uncertainty, the turn *away* was almost bound to result in loss of contact with the German fleet. A turn *towards* would have afforded protection while shortening, instead of increasing, the range. It would have been an offensive, rather than a purely defensive, movement. It is true that a turn towards enemy torpedoes subsequently became accepted practice, especially with smaller, more nimble ships. But Jellicoe had twenty-four ponderous battleships in his charge; and no one would have been more aware than he, with his mathematical mind, that the higher closing speeds of weapons and targets increase the risk of hits when a turn towards oncoming torpedoes is made. In the proposals for fighting a fleet engagement which he had previously submitted to the Admiralty, he had emphasized that he would turn away if attacked with torpedoes; his submission had been approved, and in the event he acted as he had said he would act.

Even had the Admiralty desired a bolder policy, it is doubtful if it could have been implemented. The pre-war revolution of Fisher and his group had affected only a part of the naval establishment. Fisher had forced the ships and weapons into the twentieth century: but he lacked the interest in men and means to overhaul with equal vigour the human system that would use them. Thus though Jutland was fought by a modern fleet, it was essentially a fleet governed by Victorian codes and employing tactics devised by the sea-generals of Cromwell's time. The Navy's heart was as great as ever, as the roll of personal honour emerging from the battle showed. But its head proved inadequate. The mental factor was not attuned to the nature of the fleet at its disposal. Throughout the battle, situations calling for intelligence and imagination provoked only lacunae.

In no department did this stand out more clearly than in that of reconnaissance and communication. In the vital task of passing information Commodore Goodenough alone fulfilled his function with distinction; and even he, or the signalmen involved, made a strange mistake in reporting the bearing of the German battle-cruisers at 5.50 p.m., which added to Jellicoe's perplexity at the time of deployment. Others seemed incapable of putting themselves in Jellicoe's position; of realising that, with a fleet extending over miles of sea and with visibility diminishing, he needed every scrap of guidance he could get. For the most part, questions are answered when they are asked; though the replies are sometimes far from lucid. And while the fact that radio was in its infancy must be a mitigating circumstance, the inaccuracy of signal transmission was often deplorable. As *Lion*, with her aerials shot away, was turning north Beatty semaphored to *Princess Royal*, his next astern: "Report enemy's battlefleet to C-in-C bearing S.E." This arrived on *Iron Duke's* bridge reading: "26–30 battleships, probably hostile, bearing S.S.E., steering S.E." There were in fact twenty-two battleships, and they were steering north. Had he not decided to place more faith in a message from Goodenough received a few minutes before, Jellicoe would have been seriously misled.

The failure of information reached its climax during the night. The Admiralty did not pass on to Jellicoe their knowledge that Scheer had asked for zeppelins to reconnoitre the Horns Reef area at dawn—a fairly certain clue to the route he intended to follow. And of all the British light cruisers and destroyers which subsequently clashed with the German fleet on its break-through to the east, only *Faulknor* sought to tell Jellicoe what was happening; and her signal, though repeated twice on full power, was jammed by telefunken interference. The destroyers may perhaps be exculpated: many were under deafening point-blank fire from heavy calibre guns; their gear of all kinds was being reduced to wreckage; and they were striving to hit back. But the same excuse cannot be offered in the case of the two battleships with the main fleet whose officers clearly saw one of the clashes, and noted their observations. Nor can it be maintained, as was afterwards suggested, that their silence was due to their belief that the destroyers were only beating off torpedo craft. For one of them identified "two German cruisers" with a "crane amidships," and the other a vessel with "a conspicuous crane (apparently *Westfalen* class)." Ships with large cranes could not possibly be torpedo boats, and the *Westfalen* class were well known to be battleships. Jellicoe was accused of allowing the German fleet to escape; but the blame lay more properly with the persistence of the system which rejected the unexpected, equated initiative with subversion, and regarded the inculcation of discipline as a substitute for education.

At the root of the story of expanding peoples, there is often found an instrument serving as the vehicle of their ascendency. The Roman dominance was based upon the road. The nomads of the Asian heartland rode to the plunder of the settled littorals on the dun pony of the steppes. Russia expanded to the Pacific by means of the river canoe. The European nations could colonise the world when the oared galley became the ocean-going sailing ship. Such vehicles were usually irresistible at the time of their first use; and, other things being equal, their success tended to continue until opponents could find other instruments capable of repelling them or their developments. The vehicle of Britain's ascendency was the warship, carrying her explorers and pioneers, striking down her European rivals, suppressing colonial rebellion, maintaining the seaways for her merchantmen. And as soon as the large fighting-ship evolved in the seventeenth century, this vehicle became, to all intents, the battleship. In any case, like a dinosaur faced by the evolution of more efficient animals, the battleship was doomed to extinction in the first half of the twentieth century: but Jutland hastened the process for the British battleship, because the Germans found an answer to it in its own kind. Not only did the German battleships remain sufficient in number to render the Grand Fleet's battle squadrons virtually impotent until the war was decided on land. They were also better ships.

At Jutland, 99 German ships sank nearly 112,000 tons of British metal, while 151 British ships sank 62,000 tons of German. Jellicoe's pre-war anxieties as to whether the British ships were "superior or even equal fighting machines" proved justified. The German heavy guns were of smaller calibre, yet stronger than the British; and their high muzzle velocities, ensuring even flight of shells in tightly-bunched salvoes, equalled the performance of more ponderous British weapons. German propulsion machinery occupied less space and weight, allowing the heavier protective armour and more elaborate watertight compartmenting that rendered the later German dreadnoughts almost unsinkable. The German steel was tougher, and the Zeiss optical equipment matchless in quality. The British bursting charges were inferior, as Hipper, at a hot moment of his duel with Beatty, thankfully noted; and the armour-piercing shells would often fail to penetrate when striking at oblique angles. During the battle the British fleet obtained 121 hits with heavy shells, the Germans 55: yet these 55 inflicted much more serious damage. The terrible explosions which annihilated three British battle-cruisers, Fisher's special pride, were all due to the same cause: inadequate precautions to prevent the flash from hits around the gun-turrets from spreading to the magazines below.

In British industry, and in the technical departments of the Navy responsible for its supervision, there had been grave shortcomings: lack of sound design based on factual study; lack of awareness of new materials and production methods; lack of proper testing and inspection; lack of patient modification and improvement. And this points to the underlying reason for the shock which Jutland administered to British pride. Already the balance of energy and vigour had begun to shift. Already the leadership in competitive endeavour had crossed the North Sea and was crossing the Atlantic. In a sector crucial to national survival, the onset of British decline, hidden for a generation behind the splendours of the old order, was revealed. Few recognised the deeper perspectives at the time; most were concerned to argue and explain the foreground event. But looking back at the subsequent signs and portents, at the successive stepping-stones downhill, the reality is unmistakeable.

Between the storm of bitterness that followed Jutland and the more purposeful self-criticism that marks the Britain of today—the questioning of affluence without aim; the concern for education and research; the effort to gear investment to priorities, to modernise technique and streamline management; the urge to re-kindle will, catch up again, find a new constructive role in a more dangerous yet in some respects more hopeful world—there is a direct connection. Because it seemed so indecisive, Jutland was sometimes called "the battle that was never fought." It was in fact one of the more decisive battles of modern history. For it was one of the first clear indications to Britain that the creator had become the curator.

BATTLESHIPS

2nd Battle Squadron

King George V	10	13·5-in. guns.	Vice-Admiral Sir Martyn Jerram
Ajax	10	13·5-in.	
Centurion	10	13·5-in.	
Erin	10	13·5-in.	
Orion	10	13·5-in.	Rear-Admiral A. C. Leveson
Monarch	10	13·5-in.	
Conqueror	10	13·5-in.	
Thunderer	10	13·5-in.	

4th Battle Squadron

Iron Duke	10	13·5-in.	Admiral Sir John Jellicoe
Royal Oak	8	15-in.	
Superb	10	12-in.	Rear-Admiral A. L. Duff
Canada	10	14-in.	
Benbow	10	13·5-in.	Vice-Admiral Sir Doveton Sturdee
Bellerophon	10	12-in.	
Temeraire	10	12-in.	
Vanguard	10	12-in.	

1st Battle Squadron

Marlborough	10	13·5-in.	Vice-Admiral Sir Cecil Burney
Revenge	8	15-in.	
Hercules	10	12-in.	
Agincourt	14	12-in.	
Colossus	10	12-in.	Rear-Admiral E. F. A. Gaunt
Collingwood	10	12-in.	
Neptune	10	12-in.	
St. Vincent	10	12-in.	

BATTLE-CRUISERS

3rd Battle-Cruiser Squadron

Invincible	8 12-in.	Rear-Admiral The Hon. H. L. A. Hood
Inflexible	8 12-in.	
Indomitable	8 12-in.	

ARMOURED CRUISERS

1st Cruiser Squadron

Defence Rear-Admiral Sir Robert Arbuthnot	Duke of Edinburgh
Warrior	Black Prince

2nd Cruiser Squadron

Minotaur Rear-Admiral H. L. Heath	Cochrane
Hampshire	Shannon

LIGHT CRUISERS

4th Light Cruiser Squadron

Calliope Commodore C. E. Le Mesurier	Royalist
Constance	Comus
Caroline	

Attached

Active	Boadicea
Bellona	Canterbury
Blanche	Chester

DESTROYERS

4th Flotilla

Tipperary	Broke	Ophelia
Capt. C. J. Wintour	Christopher	Owl
Acasta	Contest	Porpoise
Achates	Fortune	Shark
Ambuscade	Garland	Sparrowhawk
Ardent	Hardy	Spitfire
	Midge	Unity

11th Flotilla

Castor (light cruiser)	*Manners*	*Mons*
Commodore J. Hawksley	*Marne*	*Moon*
Kempenfelt	*Martial*	*Morning Star*
Magic	*Michael*	*Maunsey*
Mandate	*Milbrook*	*Mystic*
	Minion	*Ossory*

12th Flotilla

Faulknor	*Mary Rose*	*Nessus*
Capt. A. S. B. Stirling	*Menace*	*Noble*
Maenad	*Mindful*	*Nonsuch*
Marksman	*Mischief*	*Obedient*
Marvel	*Munster*	*Onslaught*
	Narwhal	*Opal*

OTHER SHIPS

Abdiel Minelayer
Oak Destroyer tender to Fleet Flagship

The Battle-Cruiser Fleet

Senior Officer: Vice-Admiral Sir David Beatty

BATTLE-CRUISERS

Lion 8 13·5-in. guns. Vice-Admiral Sir David Beatty

1st Battle-Cruiser Squadron

Princess Royal	8 13·5-in.	Rear-Admiral O. de B. Brock
Queen Mary	8 13·5-in.	
Tiger	8 13·5-in.	

2nd Battle-Cruiser Squadron

New Zealand	8 12-in.	Rear-Admiral W. C. Pakenham
Indefatigable	8 12-in.	

FAST BATTLESHIPS

5th Battle Squadron

Barham	8 15-in.	Rear-Admiral H. Evan-Thomas
Valiant	8 15-in.	
Warspite	8 15-in.	
Malaya	8 15-in.	

LIGHT CRUISERS

1st Light Cruiser Squadron

Galatea Cmdre. E. S. Alexander-Sinclair — *Inconstant*
Phaeton — *Cordelia*

2nd Light Cruiser Squadron

Southampton Cmdre. W. E. Goodenough — *Nottingham*
Birmingham — *Dublin*

3rd Light Cruiser Squadron

Falmouth Rear-Admiral T. D. W. Napier — *Birkenhead*
Yarmouth — *Gloucester*

DESTROYERS

1st Flotilla

Fearless (light cruiser)	Attack	Hydra
Capt. C. D. Roper	Badger	Lapwing
Acheron	Defender	Lizard
Ariel	Goshawk	

9th and 10th Flotillas (combined)

Lydiard	Laurel	Morris
Com. M. L. Goldsmith	Liberty	Termagent
Landrail	Moorsom	Turbulent

13th Flotilla

Champion (light cruiser)	Nerissa	Obdurate
Capt. J. U. Farie	Nestor	Onslow
Moresby	Nicator	Pelican
Narborough	Nomad	Petard

SEAPLANE CARRIER

Engadine

The German High Seas Fleet

Commander-in-Chief: Vice-Admiral Reinhard Scheer

BATTLESHIPS

3rd Battle Squadron

König	10 12-in. guns.	Rear-Admiral Paul Behncke
Grosser Kurfürst	10 12-in.	
Kronprinz Wilhelm	10 12-in.	
Markgraf	10 12-in.	
Kaiser	10 12-in.	Rear-Admiral Nordemann
Kaiserin	10 12-in.	
Prinz Regent Luitpold	10 12-in.	

1st Battle Squadron

Friedrich der Grosse	10 12-in.	Vice-Admiral Reinhard Scheer
Ostfriesland	12 12-in.	Vice-Admiral E. Schmidt
Thüringen	12 12-in.	
Helgoland	12 12-in.	
Oldenburg	12 12-in.	
Posen	12 11-in.	Rear-Admiral Engelhardt
Rheinland	12 11-in.	
Nassau	12 11-in.	
Westfalen	12 11-in.	

2nd Battle Squadron

Deutschland	4 11-in.	Rear-Admiral Mauve
Hessen	4 11-in.	
Pommern	4 11-in.	
Hannover	4 11-in.	Rear-Admiral F. von Dalwigk zu Lichtenfels
Schlesien	4 11-in.	
Schleswig-Holstein	4 11-in.	

LIGHT CRUISERS

4th Scouting Group

Stettin Cmdre. von Reuter	*Frauenlob*
München	*Stuttgart*
Hamburg	

DESTROYERS

Rostock (light cruiser) Cmdre. Michelson

1st Flotilla (half)	*3rd Flotilla*
4 boats	7 boats
5th Flotilla	*7th Flotilla*
11 boats	9 boats

(German destroyers were numbered, not named.)

The Battle-Cruiser Fleet

Senior Officer: Vice-Admiral Franz von Hipper

BATTLE-CRUISERS

1st Scouting Group

Lützow	8 12-in. guns.	Vice-Admiral Franz von Hipper
Derfflinger	8 12-in.	
Seydlitz	10 11-in.	
Moltke	10 11-in.	
Von der Tann	8 11-in.	

LIGHT CRUISERS

2nd Scouting Group

Frankfurt Rear-Admiral Bodicker	*Pillau*
Wiesbaden	*Elbing*

DESTROYERS

Regensburg (light cruiser) Cmdre. Heinrich

2nd Flotilla	*6th Flotilla*
10 boats	9 boats
9th Flotilla	
11 boats	

Sources

1 Admiral Sir R. Bacon, *The Jutland Scandal*. Hutchinson.

2 Quoted in Bacon, op. cit.

3 Correlli Barnett, *The Swordbearers*. Eyre and Spottiswoode, 1963.

4 *The Battle of Jutland: Official Despatches*. H.M.S.O., 1920.

5 Quoted in Geoffrey Bennett, *The Battle of Jutland*. Batsford, 1964.

6 Commander The Hon. B. Bingham, *Falklands, Jutland and the Bight*. Murray, 1919.

7 Quoted in John Buchan, *A History of the Great War* (Vol. 3). Thomas Nelson and Sons, 1922.

8 Rear-Admiral W. S. Chalmers, *The Life of Beatty*. Hodder and Stoughton, 1951.

9 Quoted in Chalmers, op. cit.

10 W. S. Churchill, *The World Crisis* (Part 1). Thornton Butterworth, 1925.

11 Sir Julian Corbett and Francis Newbolt, *Naval Operations* (Vol. 3). Longmans Green, 1923.

12 Quoted in Corbett and Newbolt, op. cit.

13 Admiral Sir Frederic Dreyer, *The Sea Heritage*. Museum Press, 1955.

14 Quoted in Dreyer, op. cit.

15 Fawcett and Hooper, *The Fighting at Jutland*. Macmillan, 1921.

16 Quoted in Fawcett and Hooper, op. cit.

17 Gorch Fock, *Nordsee*. Quoted in von Hase, *Kiel and Jutland*.

18 Lieutenant H. H. Frost, U.S.N., *The Battle of Jutland*. U.S. Naval Institute, 1936.

19 T. G. Frothingham, U.S.R., *A True Account of the Battle of Jutland*. Bacon and Bacon, Cambridge, Mass., 1920.

20 T. G. Frothingham, U.S.R., *The Naval History of the War* (Vol. 2). Cambridge, Harvard University Press, 1925.

21 German Official Record.

22 Gibson and Harper, *The Riddle of Jutland*. Cassell, 1934.

23 Quoted in Gibson and Harper, op. cit.

24 S. King Hall, *My Naval Life*. Faber and Faber, 1952.

25 Commander Georg von Hase, *Kiel and Jutland*, Skeffington and Son, 1920.

26 Admiral of the Fleet Lord Jellicoe, *The Grand Fleet, 1914–1916*. Cassell, 1919.

27 Quoted in Jellicoe, op. cit.

28 Captain Donald Macintyre, *Jutland*. Evans Brothers, 1957.

29 *Narrative of the Battle of Jutland*. H.M.S.O., 1924.

30 Quoted in *Narrative of the Battle of Jutland*.

31 *Reproduction of the Record of the Battle of Jutland*. H.M.S.O., 1927.

32 Admiral Reinhard Scheer, *The German High Seas Fleet*. Cassell, 1920.

33 Commodore G. von Schoultz, *With the British Grand Fleet*. Hutchinson, 1925.

34 *The Times*, 9 June 1916.

35 Captain von Waldeyer-Hartz, *Admiral von Hipper*. Rich and Cowan, 1933.

36 Quoted in Waldeyer-Hartz, op. cit.